East

GHOSTS

Legends
and
Lore

Peter Jeffery

LUCAS BOOKS

East Anglian
GHOSTS
Legends
and
Lore

Peter Jeffery

First Published 1988 by The Old Orchard Press
Reprinted 2006 by Lucas Books
ISBN-10   1903797-74-8
ISBN-13 9781903797-74-7

Copyright Peter Jeffery

Printed in the UK by Printwright, Ipswich

Contents

Illustrations

Introduction

*From ghoulies and ghosties and long-leggedy beasties, and
things that go bump in the night, Good Lord, deliver us!*
Things still do go bump in the night but we do not attribute
the strange and unexpected sounds to ghoulies and ghosties
and long-leggedy beasties. The days of legendary giants and
dragons are over. Their remembrance has been banished to
folklore and children's fairy tales. But tales of demonic
beasts, like the stories of ghostly monks and wicked squires,
linger with uncommon tenacity. Belief in malicious demons
and devilish phantoms declined in the 17th and 18th centuries
after the witch-hunting paranoia had been exploited by men
like Matthew Hopkins, the Witch Finder General, whose
activities resulted in hundreds of executions. Not only did the
Reformation result in the closing of the old abbeys and
priories where so many of the ghostly tales are set, but also
belief in prophecy, magic, omens and astrology faded fast.
Today, farmers will telephone the vet instead of making
offerings to St. Walstan and for toothache we consult a dentist
rather than invoking the aid of St. Apollonia and her pincers.

Yet tales of extraordinary and apparently inexplicable
encounters with spectres continue to occur. What one man
sees may well be invisible to a companion. Some who have
shared their experiences to provide material for this book
have emphasised their scepticism and even disbelief in the
reality of ghosts until it happened to them. Seeing a ghost is a
uniquely personal experience. It is unexpected and puzzling
but rarely terrifying. It is an experience which cannot be
adequately conveyed to others. I have not seen a ghost but one
October night in a very dusty and cobwebbed church tower I
certainly thought I felt the presence of something unseen. Was
it the wind in the cold spiral staircase, the occasional creak of
the ancient floor planking, or my imagination playing tricks in
the silent belfry where centuries ago a priest or sacristan went
to bed by candlelight?

Years ago in the days of carbide lamps, a policeman was
cycling along his beat one breezy night near Hopton when a

1

white, rustling apparition which changed its shape came rushing across the fields towards him. The constable, a big no-nonsense man, dropped his bicycle and hastily departed from the scene. His courage was restored at daylight and he went to retrieve his bike. He found it beside the roadside, and on top of it was the ghost - a large fertiliser bag. Many haunting stories such as this and the puzzle of the phantom footsteps in a locked church which was solved when a villager came in search of his donkey have been recounted to me. The assistance of all those who have told or re-told tales old and new is gratefully acknowledged. Regretfully modern thieves and vandals are causing more and more of East Anglia's churches to be locked, but the name of the key-holder is usually displayed. Should you seek out some of the monuments, carvings and curiosities mentioned in these pages do so with respect and care (and please shut the church doors).

Giants and the Hounds of Hell

Stories of demon dogs and giants are among the oldest and most enduring of East Anglian myths, and the roots of these tales run deep. The devilish dog, Black Shuck, is notorious throughout the region although his character varies from the benign to the deadly, depending on locality. As for giants, they are creatures as old as mythology itself.

Geoffrey of Monmouth, the 12th century writer of 'The History of the Kings of Britain', said that when Brutus and his Trojan followers landed in Britain, the island was uninhabited apart from a few giants and among this race of native goliaths was one Gogmagog who could pull up oaks with ease. Gogmagog led an attack upon the new Britons and in revenge the giants were hunted down and exterminated, except for the hideous Gogmagog. The giant was then challenged to a wrestling match by Corineus who enjoyed nothing better than grappling with 12 foot tall giants. In the struggle Corineus picked up Gogmagog and ran off with the giant over his shoulder towards a cliff overlooking the sea, from which he hurled the ugly monster to his death on the rocks below.

The scene of Gogmagog's fatal wrestling match was in the West Country a thousand years before the Christian era, according to Geoffrey of Monmouth's fanciful history, but in East Anglia the giant's name was given to the range of lows hills near Cambridge. Here Geoffrey's single giant Gogmagog became Gog and Magog, variously said to be a god and goddess of the old British tribes or a pair of giants kept as servants by Brutus in his London palace when he became king of Britain (once called Albion) ruling a population of refugee Trojans. The Gogmagog confusion is illustrated by the figures, known as Gog and Magog in London's Guildhall. Originally there were statues of the two mythical wrestlers, Gogmagog and Corineus, but they were destroyed in the Great Fire of London of 1666. The 18th century replacements became known as Gog and Magog, the last survivors of a British tribe of giants. These figures were destroyed by bombing and modern effigies of Gog and

Magog or Corineus and Gogmagog stand in their place.

Brutus, the mythical founder of Britain, is recalled in the eulogy on a warrior's tomb in the little church at Oxnead in Norfolk. Clement Paston fought England's enemies on land and sea in the service of four Tudor monarchs of Brutus' race - Henry VIII, Edward VI, Mary I and Elizabeth I. Clement made a fortune in ransom money when he captured a French admiral (a Peer of France) and brought him home in fetters.

You that beholde this statly marble tombe
And longe to knowe who here entombed lies
Here rests ye corps & shall till day of dombe
Of Clemment Paston fortunat and wise
Fourth sone to olde Sr William Paston Knight
Who dwels with God in sphere of christal bright.
Of Brutus race Princes he served fowre
In peace & warr as fortune did commaund
Sometime by sea and sometime one the shore
The Frenche and Scott he often did withstande
A pere of Fraunce in spight of all his betters
He toke in fight & brought him home in fetters.

The Gogs and nearby hills and fens abound with strange tales. The pre-Roman fort of Wandlebury dominates the Gog Magog hills and once commanded the gateway to Norfolk between the fens of Cambridgeshire and the forests of Suffolk. This stronghold of the Iceni is said to be the grave of the giants Gog and Magog and the haunt of a phantom knight. Centuries ago a figure of a giant was to be seen cut in the turf. A few miles to the north-east of Wandlebury camp, close to the ancient Icknield Way and in the centre of Fleam Dyke, is Mutlow Hill, once the place where the men of Radfield, Staine and Flendish Hundreds gathered to settle their disputes. Legend says that beneath its earth a golden chariot lies buried. Fleam Dyke, near Fulbourn, is one of a series of defensive earthworks in the area to the south of which are Brent Ditch, cut by a Roman road near Pampisford, and Bran Ditch near Fowlmere. But the mightiest is the Devil's Ditch -

who but giants or Old Nick himself could have dug such a huge defence?

The Devil's Ditch runs straight for seven miles across heathland near Newmarket, between Reach and Wood Ditton, and it perhaps marked the frontier between the kingdom of East Anglia and its aggressive neighbour Mercia. Two miles behind the line is Exning, which has several associations with early English saints - it is the traditional birthplace of St. Etheldreda who founded a monastery at Ely in 673, and is the site of St. Mindred's (or St.Wendreda's) well whose water was said to be good for the eyes.

ABOVE - *the seven miles long Devil's Ditch near Newmarket, the most massive of the giant earthworks built to protect the early kingdom of East Anglia.*

There is a very real reminder of the 'old gods' in the Wandlebury area other than the tales of dead and buried giants and their names being given to hills. On the southern face of the Norman tower of Whittlesford church is an old weathered stone carving, a Sheela-na-gig. It shows a naked and reclining female figure identified as the pagan Earth Mother goddess, and a male creature, part human, part animal. The fertility cult of the Earth Mother was widespread in the ancient world and the resemblance of Whittlesford's Sheela to a chalk figurine discovered in the Neolithic flint mines of Grimes Graves in Norfolk is startling. Some of the old fertility rites linger on in disguise - kissing under the 'sacred' mistletoe is one.

Long ago the flat, wind-blown, marshland between the Nene and the Great Ouse in west Norfolk was, according to enduring legend, the scene of such deeds of strength which only a giant of a man could have accomplished. If all the stories told of Thomas Hickathrift are to be believed then certainly he was a giant of a man. Tom was no mythical giant of pre-history like Gogmagog. The proof is in stone for all to see: upon a wall of the church of Walpole St. Peter stands a weather-worn stone effigy of a man with his hands held high above his head like a victorious boxer and that, they say, is none other than Tom Hickathrift. In the churchyard over which Tom's effigy gazes, an old notice upon a wall cautions the visitor to behave with the words -

> *The Ground Wherein thou standes is Holy Ground*
> *Let No unseemly word escape thy lips,*
> *no ill behaviour disturb God's acre.*

Another notice, this time in the porch, is a reminder of times past. It is beneath an old pair of wooden-soled shoes and states - *It is requested that all persons will take off their Pattens at the Church Door.* The 18th century novelist-earl, Horace Walpole, one of the renowned family which took its name from the village but who moved to Houghton Hall, the stately home built by his uncle, Prime Minister Robert Walpole, penned another reminder of Marshland footwear. In a letter he remarked, *We live, at least, on terra firma in this part of the world and can saunter out without stilts.*

The cathedral-like church of Walpole St. Peter has much to admire from the past - grotesque gargoyles, a graveside shelter like a sentry box for use by the priest at bad-weather burials; a Jacobean pulpit and screen; an alms box inscribed *Remember the poore 1639;* and on the chancel stalls carved reminders of East Anglia's favourite royal saint - the crowned head of St. Edmunds between the paws of a guardian wolf.

Legend does not say whether Tom Hickathrift wore pattens or used stilts when he was making his adventurous sorties around Marshland but for further 'evidence' of Tom Hickathrift you must make your way to the little village of Tilney All Saints, dominated by another of Marshlands fine medieval churches. In the churchyard beneath a huge stone, lie the bones of Tom the giant-killer and strongman, so they say, and here also stand the shafts of old, stone crosses which, of course, are really the big man's candlesticks! It would seem that a landowner called Hickafric became involved in a boundary dispute over the Smeeth, an area between Emneth and Tilney St. Lawrence When the people of the nearby villages dared to trespass on his rights, Hickafric wrenched a wheel and axletree off a cart and wielded them as he would a shield and sword to see off the invaders. This Marshland strong man's fame and prowess soon snowballed and, as in other cases, the name and legend of Tom Hickathrift has become encrusted and embellished over the centuries with stories of more and more incredible acts.

Other deeds attached to his name are great displays of strength – he would pluck up a tree for firewood - and like all legendary giants he had a gargantuan appetite for food and drink, gorging meat enough for half a dozen men and quaffing beer by the barrel. The deed that brought the greatest fame to big Tom was his slaying of a bellicose and boastful fenland giant who lived near Wisbech when in a variation of the trespass theme, Tom dared to enter the domain of the murderous cave dweller. In most British legends bad giants share several common characteristics – boastfulness and

bravado (Fee Fi Fo Fum etc.), an incredible greed for treasure and a primeval bloodthirstiness. They are portrayed as slow-witted and easily duped cave dwellers whose favourite weapon was the primitive club. In his legendary duel with the giant of Wisbech, Tom again armed himself with a wheel and axle from his wagon - they seem to have been his favourite weapons – and the lumbering, bellowing giant was very quickly battered to death. Giants, the 'bad guys' of folklore and legend, inevitably meet a bloody and violent end. These braggart giants of old England should have heeded the cautionary injunction from the book of Proverbs carved into many a churchyard headstone - *Boast not thyself of tomorrow; for thou knowest not what a day may bring forth.*

In some tales Tom Hickathrift, a food-gorging, indolent youth, grows up to become the respected sportsman adventurer, Master Thomas Hickathrift, thanks to the treasure he found in the dead giant's cave. The rags to riches theme, like that of the tale of the Pedlar of Swaffham, thus became attached to the legend of a giant-killer. The only ingredient Tom's story lacks is marriage to a beautiful princess. Sometimes Tom is depicted as a Robin Hood character siding with the poor against arbitrary authority. The manner in which Tom was said to have chosen his tomb site by hurling a stone for miles is reminiscent of the legend of Robin Hood and that of the Hertfordshire giant, Jack O'legs. Jack was a giant who also 'robbed the rich (especially the bakers of Baldock) to feed the poor' but the cunning breadmakers lured him into a trap. They blinded him and then granted him one last request before lynching him. Jack wished to be buried where his last bowshot landed and it fell to earth in Weston churchyard so that is where, it is said, one of the gentler giants of legend was laid to rest.

Another giant of a man is commemorated in the quiet Norfolk churchyard of West Somerton, little more than a mile from the coast, but in this instance there is no mystery

LEFT - *Tilney All Saints where the giant-killer Tom Hickathrift is said to be buried* surrounding his existence. He was Robert Hales who lived in the 19th century and was known as the Norfolk Giant. He grew to be 7 feet 8 inches tall, weighed 33 stones and was an innkeeper in London.

Perhaps the oddest giant of all can still be seen in an East Anglian church. He is a member of the mythical North African race of sciapodes, distinguished by their enormous webbed feet. St. Mary's church, Dennington, Suffolk, is noted for its superb 15th century carved benches with grotesque arm rests and intricate leaf decoration. On one bench end in the centre aisle is carved a member of that foreign race lying upon his back with his huge feet up in the air to shade himself from the fierce African sun. The giants of legend have proved to be mortal, be they Robin, Tom or Jack. As an old headstone at Ormesby St. Michael proclaims -

> *Death spares no sex nor Age,*
> *Sooner or later all do quit the Stage,*
> *The Old, the Young, ye Strong, ye Rich, ye Wife,*
> *Must all to him become a Sacrifice.*

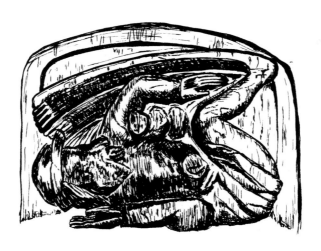

Giants and The Hounds of Hell

If you are unlucky you could encounter Black Shuck, the phantom dog which prowls by night, almost anywhere in East Anglia. He might dash past you in a lonely lane like a sudden gust of wind to send a shiver down your spine; he might stare at you from wood or hedgerow, his huge eyes ablaze with the fires of hell and his awesome fangs glinting in the moonlight; he might be seen sitting silent and motionless near a graveyard as a portent of death; or you might hear his blood-chilling howls borne on the wind. Should you consider these warnings insufficient, then heed the death and destruction visited upon Bungay and Blythburgh one summer morn in 1577 when honest men and women believed they saw the Devil appear in the form of a hell-hound amidst the flash of lightning and booming roll of thunder.

Ol' Shuck, his coat as black as a moonless midnight, is very old. The tradition of demon dogs is older than the realm of England and Shuck is probably a folktale fusion of Garm, the hound of the Underworld; Odin's black wolfhound; and Fenrir, the chained wolf of Norse mythology. Fenrir, who snapped off a god's hand in revenge for being shackled, and Garm, both wait to be freed for the last battle with the gods and warriors of Valhalla when they are destined to devour Odin and Tyr. The gods of Viking and Anglo-Saxon mythology are with us still every week of the year - Tuesday commemorates an old god of battles; Wednesday belongs to Woden, the English Odin; Thursday is Thor the Thunderer's day and Friday recalls Frigg, wife of Odin. Black Shuck of the staring, fiery eyes would have been known in some guise to Wehha, Wuffa and Tytili, the mystery-shrouded first kings of East Anglia of the early Dark Ages. Redwald, high king of Britain, son of Tytili, and the likeliest owner of the Sutton Hoo buried treasure which included a golden dragon's head, accepted Christian baptism but continued to offer sacrifices to the gods of his pagan ancestors on an altar set up alongside a Christian one.

LEFT - *the strange foreign giant in Dennington church. Shading himself beneath huge webbed feet is a sciapod carved on a medieval bench end.*

When scudding storm clouds hide the moon on a wild, winter night, that is when Odin, mounted on his eight-legged horse, Sleipnir, leads the Wild Hunt across the sky with a pack of howling hounds at his heels. When King Henry I forced the monks of Peterborough to accept one of his relatives as their new abbot in 1127, a terrifying, nocturnal wild hunt lasting for weeks greeted the unwanted man's arrival. Black huntsmen mounted upon black horses were seen and heard blowing their horns. The Anglo-Saxon Chronicle records that the fearsome hunters were accompanied by hounds as black as jet with huge, staring eyes - a whole pack of Black Shucks was at large.

Descriptions of the phantom Shuck vary depending on location. In Suffolk woodlands he is a shaggy, snarling, black wolfhound whose horrible howl is a warning of ill fortune. In Norfolk he is a silent prowler of lonely lanes with a single, blazing eye whose shrieks can be heard above the wildest storm of wind and wave. To come face to face with Shuck along the Norfolk coast is to encounter a portent of death, perhaps your own, within a twelvemonth. Elsewhere he is described as headless, or as big as a goat, or having two eyes the size of saucers that glow like burning coals. Not everywhere is this phantom to be dreaded. If meet him you must, may it be where Ol' Shuck is said to be the silent, watchful guardian against the unknown perils of the night of those who must journey between dusk and dawn.

Tales of terrifying phantom harbingers of death padding along lonely lanes and paths at night were used to advantage by men who wished their nocturnal business on deserted beaches and along the banks of rivers to be unseen by the eyes of the curious. In the 18th century smuggling was a highly organised and lucrative activity around the East Anglian coast. Kegs of rum and gin would be landed and then carted off by farm wagons or horseback to their hiding places in cottages, churches and barns. Then the tubs of spirits would be discreetly moved along the distribution network to eager customers - squire and farmer, blacksmith and country parson.

In the quiet of evening of Saturday, September 15th, 1792, James Woodforde, the rector of Weston Longville in Norfolk and compiler of a fascinating diary, received a cask of rum. The next day there were rumours of an informer and Parson Woodforde spent his Sunday evening 'much agitated' about his purchase. One way the authorities tried to curb smuggling was by encouraging informers. By an Act of Parliament the buyers of contraband were induced to name their supplier in return for having their own crime waived. Having been told that a neighbour had informed on the village blacksmith who had supplied the reverend gentleman's rum, the prudent parson rose very early on Monday and *was very busy all the Morn' in very necessary business.* He was probably engaged in doing some urgent digging in the rectory garden. A few weeks later in October the blacksmith was fined for the cask of smuggled gin found in his home by excise officers and Parson Woodforde took possession of another evening delivery of rum and brandy, gratefully tipping the carriers a shilling. He spent two hours next morning bottling the illicit spirits.

Encounters between gaugers, as excise men were known, and smugglers could be violent, as testified by two gravestones in Old Hunstanton churchyard.

*Here lie The mangled remains of Poor WILLIAM GREEN
an Honest Officer of Government Who in the faithful discharge
of his duty was inhumanly murdered by a gang of smugglers
in this Parish September 25th 1784 Aged 37 years*

The other records a shooting by smugglers the day after William Green's murder. It reads –

*In memory of William Webb Late of the 15th Lt.D'ns
who was shot from his horse by a Party of Smugglers
on the 26th of September 1784 Aged 26 Years*

Along the coast at Happisburgh the ghost of a legless seaman whose head hangs by a strip of skin between his shoulder blades is said to wander between the beach and village after dark. The sack-carrying phantom was followed one night and vanished into a well, so the next day a man was lowered down the well to investigate. He soon made a gruesome discovery - a torso with its head almost completely cut off and a pair of legs. On the beach there were signs that a gang of smugglers had fallen out over their loot and one had been murdered and his body disposed of in the well.

The most violent of the recorded sightings of the terrifying Black Dog occurred on the morning of Sunday, August 4th, 1577, not far from a favoured haunt of Suffolk smugglers. Blyford is a hamlet with church and inn at the crossroads where the lane forks to make its way across the River Blyth to Wenhaston, and tradition states that the thatched and rose-bedecked Queen's Head is at one end of a secret tunnel which goes under the road to All Saints church where a headstone carries the likeness of a Suffolk ploughman in smock and hat standing with his team. St. Peter's church, Wenhaston, surrounded by one of the loveliest churchyards in the county, has devils and demons aplenty on its 15th century Doom. This painting of judgement, with scenes of the good being received into Heaven while monsters carry off the wicked into the jaws of Hell, was discovered by accident when it was thrown out of the church during restoration work many years ago and the overnight rain removed the Puritan whitewash.

Less than two miles down river is Blythburgh and the opinion of witnesses to the events there and at Bungay more than 400 years ago was that it was not Black Shuck who visited sudden death upon the congregations of two Suffolk churches, but that it was Satan manifesting himself in canine guise.

All down the Church in midst of fire
The hellish monster flew,
And passing onwards to the Quire
He many people slew.

14

The two supposed visits by the Devil himself - no lesser demon from the fires of Hell could wreak such destruction - happened within a few minutes of each other and descriptions of what happened at Blythburgh and Bungay that summer Sunday morning are remarkably similar. Thunder and lightning proclaimed the awesome and elemental fury of the skies to herald the arrival of the Fiend. Men and women, young and old, cowered in terror as the black monster rushed among them. Within seconds the Thing departed through the Devil's Door leaving the screaming survivors to pick their way over the shattered stonework and twisted corpses which marked its path.

ABOVE - *the north door of Blythburgh church with scorch marks said to have been made by the devilish beast that caused havoc one Sunday in 1577.*

Lightning strikes on church towers are not uncommon. Dozens of East Anglian churches have been damaged by accident, collapse, storm damage or falling towers and steeples. Two hundred years after the events at Blythburgh and Bungay a violent summer storm of *lightning, hail and long continuous rain* caused the roof of the Broadland church of Billockby to crash down into the nave, smashing pews and pulpit.

The great storm that struck Blythburgh with such uncommon violence that August Sunday of 1577 occurred as the people of the village were gathered together in the church for morning worship. Towering black clouds had dimmed the light streaming in through the clerestory windows, lightning streaked from the leaden sky and the words of the lesson reader were drowned by the deafening crash of thunder. As the spire toppled through the nave roof onto the font below, the door burst open as though struck by a thunderbolt. Suddenly the fiery demon (or a second lightning strike through the gaping hole in the roof) was in the midst of the congregation. All were knocked to the ground as the devilish thing ran the length of the church. The screams of the panic-stricken were added to by the bedlam of falling timbers and shattered bells. Two lay *starke dead* - a man of 40 and a lad of 15 - as the demonic power departed. The hysterical, grovelling survivors of Blythburgh, many of them scorched by the devilish heat, slowly regained their composure to survey the sudden ruin of their church. As they did so scenes of almost identical destruction were about to be visited upon another church congregation at worship less than a dozen miles away in Bungay.

Here there was no shadow of doubt about the nature or cause of the calamity that was fast approaching out of the Suffolk skies. As the people of Bungay left their homes that morning to make their way to St. Mary's church, once a place of worship for the nuns of the convent closed after four centuries by Henry VIII, ominous storm clouds could be seen heading toward the town built in a loop of the River Waveney. The details of the terrible events which followed are contained in a pamphlet written by the Rev. Abraham Fleming of London who based his account on the words of eye-witnesses. The front of the pamphlet carries a picture of a black dog with long claws, and above are printed the words - *A straunge and terrible Wunder wrought very late in the parish church of Bongay, a Town of no great distance from the citie of Norwich, namely the fourth of this August, in ye yeere of our Lord 1577, in a great tempest of violent raine, lightning, and thunder, the like wherof hath been seldome seine. With the appeerance of an horrible shaped thing, sensibly perceived of the people then and there assembled*

As had happened in Blythburgh, the light inside the Bungay church dimmed until it was almost impossible for one person to see another and only the jagged flashes of lightning momentarily illuminated the *palpable darknesse*. The rolling rumble of thunder grew so violent and forceful that the people were *perplexed in minde and at their wits' end*. Torrents of rain lashed down to add to the growing fear of the congregation as *senseless things void of all life and feeling shook and trembled*. The church was enveloped by *a great, terrible and fearful tempest. . such darkness, rayne, hayle, thunder & lightnyng as was never seen the lyke*. The hearts of all were struck by a sore and sudden fear as the ground trembled and the thick walls shook.

Then entered the *horrible shaped thing*. It was a black dog, or, as many believed at the time, the Devil disguised as one. Certainly it was no demented animal driven to seek shelter in the church by the violence of the storm outside - this beast had eyes of fire and it killed and burned any person in its path. With incredible speed it dashed among the kneeling congregation, passing between two men it *wrung the necks of them bothe at one instant cleane backward, insomuch that even at a moment where they kneeled they strangely dyed*. Evidence of the scorching heat generated by the monstrous intruder was the injury to another man who was seized *in such a gripe on the back, that therewithal he was presently drawen togither and shrunk up, as it were a peece of lether scorched in a hot fire*. This victim *dyed not*. The church escaped major damage but the clock's wheels and wires were left twisted and broken.

Greater hurt was caused when fire destroyed the town in 1688. *Upon Friday the first of March last, about Sun-rising, there happed in the Town of Bungay in Suffolk a sad and furious Fire, whereby in the space of six hours the Great Church, which was an eminent Fabrick, was destroyed, and near Two Hundred Families are bereft of habitation; And several great Brewing Offices, Ware Houses, Shops, Barnes, Stables, and other Out-Houses and Building, near Four Hundred in Number beside Three Almes-Houses, with several Apartments, Two famous Market-Crosses and the Shambles, are laid in Ashes and heaps of Ruine.* Appeals for help were sent out because *many that lived in good Fashion saved nothing but the Cloaths on their Backs. The Desolation is most lamentable, and the loss is estimated by them that speak modestly at Thirty Thousand Pounds.* The industrious folk of Bungay raised a new town upon the ashes of the old as their neighbours at Beccles had done after God's heavie wrath in fiery flame had visited that town on St. Andrew's Eve, 1586. Another devilish tradition lingers in St. Mary's churchyard, Bungay. At the western end stands the Druid's Stone around which one must dance a dozen times to summon forth the Prince of Darkness.

The great arc carved by the Waveney made Bungay an enticing site for a castle and the troublesome Bigod Earls of Norfolk obliged by building a mighty fortress of stone from which they could defy royal authority. Stephen and Henry II both attacked its walls to curb that insolent and overmighty vassal, Hugh Bigod who had no compunction about changing allegiance if he considered it to be to his advantage.

In 1173 Hugh, well over 70 years old, rebelled against his king and was bottled up in his Bungay castle. The walls were undermined and the old baron had to surrender, and, to keep his castle on the Waveney, the bold earl had to renew his oath of fealty and pay 1,000 marks, or as an old ballad says, three score sacks of gold.

Giants and The Hounds of Hell

When news was brought to London town
How Sir Bigod did jest and sing,
'Say you to Lord Hugh of Norfolk,'
Said Henry, our English King,
'Though you be in your Castle of Bungay,
Upon the River of Waveney
I'll make you care for the King of Cockney!'

King Henry he marshal'd his merry men all,
And through Suffolk they march'd with speed;
And they march'd to Lord Bigod's castle wall,
And knocked at his gate, I rede;
'Sir Hugh of the Castle of Bungay,
Upon the River of Waveney,
Come doff your hat to the King of Cockney.'

Sir Hughon Bigod, so stout and brave,
When he heard the King thus say,
He tumbled and shook like a May-mawther,
And he wish'd himself away:
'Were I out of my Castle of Bungay,
And beyond the River of Waveney,
I would ne care for the King of Cockney.'

Sir Hugh took three score sacks of gold,
And flung them over the wall;
Says 'Go your ways, in the Devil's name,
Yourself and your merry men all!
But leave me my Castle of Bungay,
Upon the river of Waveney,
And I'll pay my shot to the King of Cockney!'

Henry II was not one to forgive and forget, even for 1,000 marks. When Hugh died the earldom was withheld from the old baron's son and heir Roger, who had to wait a decade until England had a new royal master before succeeding to the title. Like the nunnery founded by Hugh's wife, Bungay castle is now a ruin. Black Shuck, they say, has been seen near the old

castle walls - or is it the ghost of the bold but humbled Bigod who once boasted that he *would ne set a button by the King of Cocknaye?*

Blythburgh, too, has its own ghost story as well as associations with the hack and clash of ancient battle. Not a mile south of the church is an area known as Toby's Walks, now a picnic site. It is said to be haunted by the ghost of a soldier who was hanged for murder more than two centuries ago. Tobias Gill was a drummer with a cavalry regiment in the army of King George II. Perhaps the troops were there to discourage the smugglers of Blyford and Walberswick. Be that as it may, soldier Toby got drunk one night and as he staggered across the Common he encountered a servant girl who was found dead the next morning.

Toby was accused of the girl's death, convicted of murder and hanged close to the scene of the crime, beside the road where the old mail coaches climbed the hill on their way towards Yoxford and Saxmundham. As the east winds of winter swept across the marshes behind Dunwich to rattle the chains encasing Toby's bones, a new tale of terror was born. In the hours of darkness, it was said a phantom coach had been seen, drawn by four headless horses frantically whipped along on their hellish journey by a ghostly figure which had been recognised as none other than Black Toby, doomed forever to drive the spectral coach-and-four along Tinker's Walk. What better tale could have been concocted to allow the smugglers of Sole Bay to pursue their nocturnal enterprises undisturbed?

Five centuries before Henry Plantagenet confronted the Norman earl, Hugh Bigod, on the banks of the Waveney, and almost a thousand years before the terrible Black Dog storm struck Blythburgh and Bungay, a fierce and deadly clash took place beside the river Blyth. With the death of Redwald in 625

LEFT - *St. Mary's church, Bungay, where death and destruction were said to have been caused by a horrible black dog during a violent storm in 1577.*

the power of his dynasty and kingdom went into decline and many East Anglian kings died at the hands of heathen invaders. The saintly Sigebert, who gave up the crown for the life of a monk in the monastery he had founded at Bury St. Edmunds, was persuaded to lead an army against the pagan Penda of Mercia. Refusing to bear arms, he was killed wielding only a stick. Anna, the father of five or six saints, became king but he, too, fell in battle with Mercian swords at Bulcamp in 654. Anna's body, with that of another battle victim, St. Jurmin, said to have been the king's son, were carried a mile to the Saxon church at Blythburgh for burial. Centuries later when abbots went to extraordinary lengths to enlarge their monastic collections of holy relics, the bones of king and saint were carried off to the great abbey at Bury St. Edmunds. The two black stones in the floor near the font at Blythburgh may have marked the royal tombs during their sojourn beside the Blyth.

The steeple which fell into the church during the thunder storm of 1577 was never replaced and the demonic fireball, or whatever it was, thankfully, spared Blythburgh's wonderful carvings. Wooden effigies of King Anna and his saintly daughter, Etheldreda of Ely, are among the apostles and saints fronting the chancel stalls; on the nave benches are reminders of worldly vices - greed and gluttony, sloth and slander among them - and in the roof flights of wide-winged angels which, as in other churches, became the targets of Puritan gunmen. But even as the fine medieval building which houses them was being completed in 1492 the fortunes of the community it was to serve were in decline because the new, larger ships could not sail up the river, so the shipbuilding tradesmen deserted the town. The 12th century priory, whose monks had started the building of the church, was suppressed, its buildings left to crumble and vanish, and the great parish church itself suffered neglect, decay and deliberate desecration before rescue work began late in the 19th century. As evidence that the destruction visited upon Blythburgh and Bungay churches was diabolically inspired rather than the result of natural forces, it was said that the devilish beast left its claw marks on the doorways. But many a church door arch has been gouged by careless accident during the passing years. At Blythburgh some burn marks, said to have been made by the fiery intruder, mark the north or Devil's door. In some churches the north door is often called the Devil's door because of the old superstition that it should remain open during baptism to allow evil spirits to escape. Fire from the sky, sometimes in the form of German bombs, has hit churches in Norwich, South Walsham, Beccles, Creeting All Saints, and other East Anglian towns and villages, but, as when Flixton church lost its roof in a hurricane, no demonic dog was blamed. Neither was a dog cited for the destruction in Danbury church during a violent storm long ago when a man died from burns - his legs and feet turned black. But they did say the Devil was seen disguised in the hood and habit of a monk.

ABOVE - *The ruins of 'the Castle of Bungay upon the River of Waveney', once the stronghold of the troublsome Hugh Bigod, Earl of Norfolk.*

ABOVE - *Blythburgh's fine church which lost its spire in a legendary storm. The church is renowned for its medieval carvings of the Seven Deadly Sins.*

Dragons Dreadful and Dragons Dozy

Tales of dragons have been familiar to the people of East Anglia for centuries. An eighth century epic poem tells how Beowulf was mortally wounded by a fire-breathing dragon which guarded a hoard of buried treasure. The description of the hero-king's fiery funeral brings to mind the Anglo-Saxon treasures discovered at Sutton Hoo. Old manuscripts written by medieval monks tell other tales of dragons, on occasion the monstrous creatures had been seen languidly basking in the summer sunshine or, when in meaner mood, killing sheep, and terrorising villages.

ABOVE - *St. George depicted on the 15th century screen in Ranworth church.*

25

Stories of these fearsome beasts had been told and retold in church and cottage for generations. The kings of England adopted St. George, the most famous of all dragon-killers, as the nation's patron and guardian, and since the time of the Crusades his popularity had greatly increased, particularly among knights and soldiers.

The saint's brave exploit was colourfully portrayed for all to see in the painted pictures on church walls, in the glass of windows and the carved woodwork. So, too, was the story of another popular figure, St. Margaret of Antioch, who was believed to have been swallowed by a dragon from which she miraculously escaped when the vile beast burst! Her cult was particularly honoured in Norfolk and Suffolk. With such tales of saints and dragons so well known, the men and women of East Anglia would certainly have recognised a dragon when they saw one.

Late in the 12th century a dragon was reported to be causing mayhem in the Essex countryside where the Saxon princess and saint, Osyth, had founded a convent and where a monastery was later built for monks charged with the care of her shrine. This fiery dragon at St. Osyth was described as being 'of marvellous bigness' so much so that it demolished houses in its path. The apparent predilection of dragons for living close to rivers and creeks, and taking their ease in the sunshine is illustrated by the tale of the beast that brought fear to the Broadland village of Ludham. There a winged monster would emerge from its lair each evening to cause the good people of Ludham to hasten home to endure a fearful, self-imposed curfew behind barred doors while the dreadful beast prowled river bank, marsh and village during the long, nocturnal hours until dawn. Then, as the sun rose, the dragon would disappear into its subterranean retreat. Repeatedly the villagers blocked the mouth of the tunnel, but each evening the beast would burst through their barricade. One day the dragon came out of its lair to enjoy the warm, sunny weather and as the monster lazily dozed, a resourceful villager rolled a huge stone over the entrance. When the dragon returned it could not shift the impediment and flew into an enraged fury and, snorting and bellowing its frustration and anger, the hellish creature lumbered off across the marshes to St. Benet's Abbey beside the River Bure where it vanished, never again to disturb the lives of the citizens of Ludham. A red dragon can still be seen in Ludham standing upon its hind legs, accompanied by a crowned lion, supporting the heraldic arms of Queen Elizabeth I in the chancel arch of St. Catherine's church. Below them are the words *Non Me Pudet Evangelii Christi (I am not ashamed of Christ's Gospel) Vivat Regina Elizabeta*.

Two stories of dragon activity in the Stour Valley were recorded during the 15th century. In 1405 a dragon with a huge body, crested head, sharp teeth and a long tail appeared on the lands of Sir Richard de Waldegrave's manor at Bures. When the beast began killing sheep the men of Bures grabbed their longbows and showered the dragon with arrows. Their aim was good, but the arrows bounced harmlessly off the dragon's thick skin. Disconcerted by the ineffectiveness of their missiles, the archers awaited the arrival of more armed men from neighbouring parishes. Soon the reinforcements arrived but when the dragon saw this small but valiant army of countrymen advancing to the attack again, it discreetly retreated into a nearby mere where it disappeared among the reeds never to be seen again. No doubt the men of Bures gave thanks for their victory in the village church with its old wooden effigy of a mail-clad knight with sword and shield, and font adorned with the arms of the Waldegraves and other noble families.

Almost half a century elapsed before the peace of the Stour Valley was disturbed again by dragons and this time the scene of the commotion was just north of Bures in the neighbouring parish of Little Cornard. It was a period of prosperous peace in Suffolk thanks to the wool trade, and the Wars of the Roses, which were to cost King Henry VI both his crown and his life, were hidden in the unknown future. By 1449 the long wars in France were at an end, the King and Queen had founded new colleges at Cambridge, the wealthy merchants of Lavenham and Long Melford would soon build fine new churches and in the villages of England the harvest had been safely gathered in. But that year, on the evening of September 26th, the feast day of two more legendary saints of Antioch, Cyprian and Justina, the rural calm of Little Cornard was shattered by two dragons locked in deadly combat.

The River Stour divides the counties of Suffolk and Essex and on its eastern side is Kedington Hill and to the west the higher Ballingdon Hill. With much biting and clawing and lashing of tails the two dragons were engaged in a ferocious duel in a marshy field known as Sharpfight Meadow. The people of Cornard hastened to the scene where the broadening river curves into Essex. On the other bank, also enjoying the curious spectacle were people from Lamarsh, Great Henny and Middleton. Perhaps amid that throng were some grey-haired veterans of that earlier dragon fight at Bures. This was to be no brief encounter on the reedy banks of the Stour. The confrontation between the black dragon of Kedington Hill and the spotted red beast of Ballingdon Hill was long and bitter. For an hour they snapped and snarled, growled and grappled until eventually the battered black creature was vanquished. Then the two exhausted dragons lumbered slowly away, ignoring the amazed human spectators, and disappeared into the two hills overlooking the placid waters of the Stour. This bizarre battle is recorded in an old document preserved in Canterbury Cathedral. Another venomous flying serpent is said to have killed many inhabitants of Saffron Walden before a brave knight despatched the monster. A more docile dragon was spotted a few miles away at Henham, according to a 17th century pamphlet writer. After stretching out in the sun the big-eyed beast disappeared into a wood.

Dragons depicted by medieval artists can still be seen in several East Anglian churches. Among the best are - Fritton, Norfolk, a wall painting of St. George on a white horse about to slay a prostrate dragon; Wellingham, Norfolk, screen dated 1532 has a painting of St. George in similar pose to that at Fritton being watched by king and queen from a nearby castle and sacrificial princess with a lamb; Bradfield Combust, Suffolk, wall painting of St. George killing a dragon with sword and lance; Ranworth, Norfolk, screen shows a curiously armed St. George standing upon a rather feeble looking blue-backed dragon; Withersfield, Suffolk, has a bench carving of a monstrously grotesque dragon being charged by a mounted St. George with a lance, and at Thornham Parva, Suffolk, the beautiful 14th century retable shows St. Margaret of Antioch spearing a writhing dragon with its tail in knots. Heraldic dragons are also shown on the Elizabethan royal arms at Tivetshall St. Margaret, Preston and Kenninghall (an arrow-tongued spotty monster). A 15-foot-long dragon once used in pageants is in Norwich Castle Museum.

Wild and Wicked Men, Children Green and Tragic

Around the time that cantankerous old earl, Hugh Bigod, was being brought to heel by his sovereign, King Henry, in his Bungay stronghold, the people along the Suffolk coast at Orford had something strange to talk about. Like Blythburgh and Walberswick, Southwold and Dunwich, the prosperity which once came to Orford's port in the holds of merchant ships has vanished. The East Coast tides that swept away the streets, churches, homes and shops of Dunwich have piled up a shingle beach ten miles long to force the River Alde to make a great southerly detour before it can reach the sea. In 1165, when the turncoat Bigod was building his keep at Bungay, Henry II began the construction of a new fortress at Orford in the hope that it would put a stop to the plots of the treacherous earl. Henry's castle marked the introduction of new ideas in castle design - the keep has projecting towers to make the defenders' fire more effective - and it was finished just in time to withstand a siege by an army of rebels led by Hugh Bigod.

But it was not the building or the siege of the king's new castle which made the abbot-chronicler, Ralph of Coggeshall, take a curious interest in the events at the Suffolk port. His attention was attracted by the strange tales people were telling of the hairy wild man the local fishermen had pulled from the sea. The man-like creature had been trapped in the seamen's nets, brought ashore and turned over to the custody of the castle commander, Bartholomew de Glanville. The naked captive had a long, pointed beard and his body was covered by shaggy hair and his head was almost bald. The castellan had his strange charge locked up to prevent escape and noted the wild man's greedy appetite for raw fish which were squeezed dry before being consumed. Except for a few grunts and moans the unfortunate prisoner remained silent and even when he was strung up by his feet and cruelly tortured he would not, or could not, utter an intelligible word in answer to the insistent questioning by his interrogators.

ABOVE - *The stone keep of Orford castle with a cannon in the foreground. It was in the 12th century fortress built by King Henry II that the wild man from the sea caught in nets by Orford fishermen was imprisoned and interrogated.*

He was taken to Orford's Norman church but neither the building not its holy objects were greeted by the slightest gesture of reverence or recognition. The wild man knew nothing of religion. One day nets were stretched across the harbour and the wild man was allowed to return to the waters. The precautions proved useless. He dived deep under the three lines of nets and re-appeared in the sea beyond to begin a derisive display of swimming and diving as if taunting the human spectators on the beach. Then, unexpectedly, he returned to his captors to resume his life on land. As the weeks passed the curiosity value of the wild man from the sea declined, and the castle guards relaxed their vigilance. But the wild man became disenchanted with his confined life on land. Then, one day, he sneaked away to the beach and vanished forever beneath the waves. Abbot Ralph recorded the story more than half a century after the event but whether the wild man of Orford was a man, a fish, or an evil spirit in the corpse of a dead man he could not say.

Wild and Wicked Men, Children Green and Tragic

Orford's importance as a port disappeared as the shingle spit of Orford Ness grew longer. The castle keep became an obsolete monument to the old quarrels between kings and barons, and the church's Norman chancel arcade, built about the same time as the castle, fell into ruin. The top of the tower fell in 1830 but has been rebuilt and the church is noted for its carved font and civilian brasses showing changes in fashion between the Wars of the Roses and the Civil War. East Anglia's tradition of wild men is not, however, confined to Orford. The idea of wild men and fearsome beasts lurking in forests and dark, deserted places is echoed in many tales from ancient mythology, and in children's fairy tales forests are the lairs of evil old witches, dwarves and 'the Jabberwock with eyes of flame'.

The wild man of the woods, long-haired and bearded, wearing the skins of animals and, like many giants, armed with a club, found his way into many old churches. Often he is shown carved in stone around the stems of fonts - perhaps he was put there to frighten away evil spirits or could it be that like the Green Man he is a symbol of the renewal of life? The woodwose or wild man of church iconography may have descended from ancient pagan fertility beliefs.

Among the churches where woodwose can be seen around the font are Happisburgh in Norfolk and Middleton in Suffolk, and on the porch of Yaxley church two wild men fight beasts. At St. Margaret's, King's Lynn, where a storm brought down the spire in 1741, a Green Man appears on the chancel stalls with King Edward III, Queen Philippa, their son, the Black Prince, and the fighting bishop of Norwich, Henry Dispenser, who wielded a sword with effect in crushing the Peasants Revolt of 1381. Another Green Man is in Ely Cathedral, his face surrounded and part hidden by the foliage pouring out of his mouth. At Norton in Suffolk woodwose are on the font and another is being eaten by a lion on a misericord near a less fanciful carving of a woman chastising a child's bare rump.

LEFT - *wild men or woodwose carved on the fonts at Happisburgh and Orford.*

More than 600 years ago an unknown graffiti artist etched the picture of a very strange creature into a pillar of St. Mary's church, Beechamwell, in Norfolk's Breckland. Known as the Beechamwell Demon, the scratched drawing shows a human-like body with a grotesque, shaggy face, horns, animal ears and a long tongue protruding out of its mouth and in its left hand it holds a tree branch. The little thatched church, set on a green in the middle of the village, has a round Saxon tower with a later octagonal top stage and to the west and south are the ruins of a trio of other old churches. At Westley Waterless, Cambridgeshire, where a murderer on the run took sanctuary in 1364 and left behind his sword, bow and arrows worth 2s 6d when he was exiled, someone, probably the priest, recorded the grape harvest from 11 vines by scratching the totals into the soft stone around a window. Perhaps the priest of Westley was producing his own wine for Mass and, perchance, among those who tasted it were Sir John de Creke, one time Sheriff of the county, and his wife Alyne, whose memorial brasses in the church are two of the very finest in the land. The brasses, 650 years old, show Sir John armed and accoutred as if to ride to war and his lady in graceful gown, cloak and wimple. When Sir John acquired the manor of Westley, the church had a round Saxon tower but it fell down in the 19th century and now the little church of St. Mary the Less where once, perhaps, grapes grew up its flint walls, a single chime is housed in a small bellcote. Other stone-scratchers have carved an archer at Whittlesford, windmills at Dalham, crusader crosses at Worlington and a ship at Cowlinge. A reminder that in the past churches were often used as schoolrooms is at Blythburgh where the choirstalls have holes for inkwells and a young Swede unable to comprehend his lessons, incised the words *DIRCK LOWERSEN VAN STOCKHOLM ANNO 1665.*

RIGHT - *the effigy of a knight holding a heart in his hands in Wickhampton church. An old story says he was turned to stone by God as an example to wrong-doers.*

Wild and Wicked Men, Children Green and Tragic

Why medieval craftsmen carved hideous creatures into benches and roofs, fashioned wild men on fonts, and demons and ugly faces around walls no-one can be sure. Were the bench monsters of Mendlesham, Stowmarket, Wordwell, and Gateley warnings of the hellish torments that awaited sinners or the innocent products of over-imaginative carpenters? Were the ugly tongue-pokers, monsters, dragons, demons and nightmarish gargoyles high up on exterior walls fashioned by superstitious artisans in the belief that they would keep evil spirits at bay or as reminders that human passions should be left at the door of God's house? Their significance is a mystery, as it was 850 years ago to the learned Abbot of Clairvaux who became St. Bernard.

Wickhampton is now a quiet Norfolk hamlet of church, farm and houses on the edge of the marshes that stretch eastward to the junction of the rivers Waveney and Yare where once Roman warships anchored safely below the strong walls of Burgh Castle. Wickhampton was a tiny place when it became a small part of William of Normandy's prize for his victory over a stubborn English army on Senlac Hill one October day in 1066. As the village grew so did its church of St. Andrew and in the oldest part of the building, the 12th century chancel, is the effigy of a knight around which a strange, bloody and cautionary tale of God's wrath developed.

Set into the north wall beneath canopied arches of carved stone are the tombs of Sir William Gerbrygge and his wife upon which are the effigies of a knight in chain mail armour and surcoat of the late 13th century and his lady in gown, headdress and wimple with her hands together in prayer. For 700 years and more the two figures have lain with their proud displays of armorial shields. Their paint has gone with the passing centuries and now they bear the initials of later irreverent graffiti-scratchers. The detail, however, which inspired the strange story of a deadly duel is the heart of stone which Sir William clasps to his breast between the palms of his hands, an unusual but not unique feature because in the church at East Tuddenham Sir Edmund Berry is shown with his heart in his hands.

Sir William Gerbrygge lived at the time when King Edward I was conquering Wales and carrying war north of the border into Scotland. Maybe his name and generous patronage had been long forgotten when the tale was first told of how a stone knight holding his heart in his hands came to be in the little church of Wickhampton. Long ago, the tradition says, two brothers were the masters of two neighbouring parishes but each sought to secure an advantage over the other. They disputed the boundary between their lands and eventually their quarrel became so fierce and passionate that the brothers fought a bloody and maniacal duel in which each tore the beating heart from the body of his opponent. This savagery aroused God's anger to such a degree that He decided to make a lasting example of them as a warning to others who might be tempted into acts of wickedness. He turned them both to stone and placed them in the church for all to see with their hearts clutched in their hands. The surname of the wicked pair was given to the village where they lie - Wicked Hampton, which, as the years passed, became shortened to Wickhampton while the other parish, known as Hell Fire Gate, evolved into Halvergate a mile to the north.

Disputes over the ownership of land were not rare when wealth and prestige among the nobility and knights of the shires was founded on manorial rights. Sir John de Creke, that knight depicted in brass at Westley Waterless, is said to have successfully defended the claims of his manor in a duel fought against Sir Thomas de Burgh of neighbouring Burrough Green. Sir Thomas was also subjected to the malice of his sister who tried to get her hands on his estates by claiming that he was not the true father of his children. But Thomas's son John did inherit, and made peace with his grasping aunt before passing his patrimony to his brother and departing to a monastery. An effigy of the forgiving monk is among those of the once mighty de Burghs in St. Augustine's church with its curiously roofed aisle.

Near a crossroads on the road which leads from Norwich to the coast at Blakeney a stone marks the spot where the heated and quarrelsome words uttered at an election resulted in a fatal duel fought by Sir Henry Hobart, fourth baronet of the Blickling Hall dynasty founded by a Stuart Lord Chief Justice. Sir Henry, who had supported the overthrow of James II, crossed swords on Cawston Heath with Oliver Le Neve of Great Witchingham Hall on August 20th, 1698. Le Neve ran his sword through the body of his aristocrat opponent who was carried back to Blickling where he died of his wounds the following day. The victor of the encounter hastily took ship across the North Sea to safety in Holland but later he returned to stand trial for murder and was acquitted of the charge. Close to the spot where Sir Henry suffered his fatal wound is Cawston's church of St. Agnes where a mythical woodwose and dragon guard a piscina and the screen of painted saints includes a rare picture of John Shorne, the 13th century priest and cult figure whose help was sought by sufferers of gout and who was credited with holding the Devil captive in a boot. A reminder of a more convivial and amiable past activity than duelling is the inscription near the tower *God spede the plow and send us ale corn enow our purpose for to make* ... The purpose was to make beer which financed the building of the church tower. Better to be *marry and glede* at a church ale than duelling and dead!

Wickhampton's church houses other old treasures apart from the stony likeness of Sir William Gerbrygge with a heart in his hands. On the north wall of the nave are some of the finest medieval wall paintings in East Anglia including the macabre tale imported from France of the 'Three Living and Three Dead'. This story of three kings enjoying the worldly pleasures of the hunt when they are suddenly confronted by a trio of skeletons as a reminder that Death awaits them appealed to the medieval mind and was painted on the walls of many churches. The skeletal trio gave the three carefree monarchs a jolting warning that none, rich or poor, prince or pauper, can escape the inevitable grave.

Variations of the phrase 'As I am now so shall you be' are common among the ominous admonitions to be seen on churchyard headstones and tombs. In Norwich cathedral a skeleton on a wall where *THOMAS GOODING HERE DO STAYE WA YTING FOR GOD'S JUDGEMENT DAYE* is accompanied by the words -

> *All you that do This place pass bye*
> *Remember death for you must Dye*
> *As you are now Even so was I*
> *And as I am so shal you be.*

At Arkesden an ornate and proud Elizabethan monument has the effigies of Richard Cutte and his wife Mary, whose father *was chiefe butler of England to the most renounded king Edward the 6*. Around the tomb are their weeping offspring, some beheaded, and the words *As ye nowe are, so once weare we, As we nowe are, so shall ye be. When ye remember us, forget not your selves.*

Just as the legend of the Three Living and Three Dead was painted big and bold on church walls as pictorial warnings which could be understood by the illiterate men and women of medieval England, so headstones could carry a message of caution to the more widely educated generations of later years. A ledger slab in the cloister of Norwich cathedral in memory of a merchant gives another variation of the theme that the Great Reaper may call without warning-

> *Reader, an unexpected stroke of death*
> *May soon deprive thee of thy fleeting breath.*

At Tibenham a verse similarly warns how quickly Death may strike the unwary -

> *Oh! let my sudden doom*
> *A warning be to all*
> *E'en while thou bendest o'er my tomb*
> *Thou may'st as quickly fall.*

And at Geldeston -

> *Death does not always Warning give*
> *Therefore be Careful how you live.*

At Seething, the thatched and round-towered church has its own painting of the Three Living and Three Dead as well as other 14th century wall paintings and a headstone from the early 19th century urging the reader to instant contrition -

> *All you that Come my Grave to see,*
> *As I am now so must you be.*
> *Therefore Repent, make no Delay*
> *For I was quickly snatch'd away.*

As good a warning as any to the complacent is the doggerel verse to a young man at North Cove where wall paintings 700 years old show angels sounding trumpets, the dead emerging from their coffins and the wicked being ushered into the jaws of hell -

Art thou in health and spirits gay,
Ah so was I the other day;
And thought my self of life as safe,
As you that read my epitaph.

Also on the wall of Wickhampton church is a huge painting of St. Christopher, the patron of travellers, who was a popular medieval figure because of the superstition that those who saw his likeness would suffer no harm that day. In many churches a large picture of the saint wading through a river with the infant Christ held high on his shoulder is the first thing to be seen on entry. St. Christopher was said to have been a pagan giant who forsook the Devil and carried travellers across a dangerous river. Pictures of the saint can be seen at Bradfield Combust and Grundisburgh, Suffolk; Little Baddow, Essex; Seething and Hardley, Norfolk, and a particularly colourful one at Willingham near Cambridge. A 20th century version with car and aeroplane is in Lound's 'Golden Church'.

The most interesting of Wickhampton's wall art are the Seven Acts of Mercy - a series of pictures in comic strip fashion illustrating deeds such as giving food to the hungry, clothing the naked, comforting the sick and visiting a captive who is shown in the stocks. Among the other subjects painted by medieval church artists were St. Francis preaching to the birds as at Wissington; the Virgin Mary and Holy Child at Belchamp Walter and Gt. Canfield; St. Edmund at Lakenheath and Fritton, Suffolk; the tree of seven deadly sins with dragon heads and demons, and Christ of the Trades with old tools and the six of diamonds playing card at Hessett; and Thomas Becket at Hauxton. The restored 12th century paintings in Copford's Norman church give an idea of how colourful were English pre-Reformation church interiors.

Elizabeth I ordered 'pictures and other like fancies' to be replaced by biblical texts so they disappeared under coats of lime wash to await discovery in later centuries. Edifying texts replaced the figures and, around the time of Will Shakespeare's birth, the priest of Weston in Suffolk chose some words of St. Paul to get his message across - *Let him that is taught in the word, make him that hath taught him, partaker of all his goods.* Perhaps some tithes were overdue!

ABOVE - *the Boy's Grave near Newmarket, said to be the crossroads burial site of a young shepherd boy who committed suicide over a missing lamb. The colours of the flowers on the grave are claimed to indicate winning racehorses.*

Tucked into the north-east corner of a crossroads where a lane to Chippenham is cut by the old road between Newmarket and Bury St. Edmunds, is a grave often adorned with flowers. Some people would have you believe that here lie the earthly remains of 'Joseph the Unknown Gypsy Boy', but whether the bones that are buried there - if there are any bones at all - belonged to a young gypsy or anyone else who went by the name of Joseph nobody knows. It is a mystery which has spawned tales both plausible and fanciful. If the story of a needless and tragic youthful suicide has a kernel of truth, then the events which resulted in the Boy's Grave must have happened around 200 years ago or more.

'Joseph' - the name is a modern fiction - is said to have been a young shepherd boy or gypsy who either miscounted his sheep or found his flock one short and, fearing the consequences because sheep-stealing was then a capital offence, he took his own life. In one version a melodramatic ending is given to the tale by the stray animal safely reappearing with the new dawn, too late to prevent tragedy because during the night the boy had hanged himself. At that time the bodies of suicides were denied burial in a churchyard, so 'Joseph' was interred at a four-way crossroads in the belief that his restless spirit would not wander abroad to the alarm of the living because it would not know which path to take - north, south, east or west. By the mid-19th century the number of capital offences, particularly those of minor theft, had been greatly reduced and churchyards made provision for the graves of suicides, albeit in unhallowed ground.

For years flowers have bloomed on the Boy's Grave but nobody knew how they came to be there - was it the work of sentimental travellers, or passing Romany wayfarers remembering one of their own? On most mornings thoroughbred racehorses from Newmarket's racing stables gallop across the heathland not very far from the grave and this proximity has bred the Derby Day myth that the colours of the flowers on the grave that day are those worn by the jockey destined to win the great race. Alternatively, say some, the blooms indicate success for a Newmarket horse in a Classic race on the town's Rowley Mile course which is named after Old Rowley, the favourite mount of King Charles II.

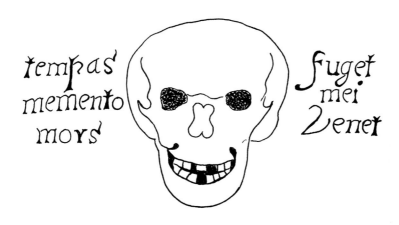

tempas memento mors

fuget mei Denet

ABOVE - *skull and memorial slab of the mid-17th century set in the floor of Heckingham church.*

A legend of much older ancestry involving bewildered youngsters is that told of the two green children who appeared out of the ground into the bright light of day at Woolpit in Suffolk. As in the case of Orford's wild man from the sea, the story was recorded by Ralph of Coggeshall and another chronicler, William of Newburgh, tells the same tale in his writings in which he admits that his initial scepticism of such an apparently ridiculous 'marvel' was overwhelmed by the evidence of so many credible witnesses. William says that the strange events, the like of which had been unheard of since time began, happened during the reign of King Stephen, 1135-54, when the two children appeared from the old wolfpits which gave the village its name. They were found wandering confused and perplexed through the fields by villagers gathering the corn. What the harvesters were most astonished to discover about the distraught brother and sister was not their unintelligible speech or strange clothing but the fact that, from head to toe, their skin was green. As the news spread people hastened to Woolpit to gaze upon the young aliens who, although they were obviously famished, steadfastly refused any of the various foods offered them. They were taken to the home of Sir Richard de Calne where they chanced to see some bean pods fresh from the fields and indicated that this was their kind of food. Soon the beans were shelled for the young couple to eagerly consume. With the passage of time the flesh of the children lost its green hue, they learned the language of their new guardians and even developed a taste for new foods. The boy, who was the younger of the two, became melancholy and morose in his new surroundings and died. The girl, however, was soon just like other girls and became a servant in the knight's household for some years until she left to be married at King's Lynn.

Where had these children of green complexion come from? They said they lived in 'St. Martin's Land' where everyone and everything was green. St. Martin was the most revered of the saints in their land which they described as a place where the sun never rose, a twilight land where the light of day was like the dim of dawn or dusk. But not far from this shadowy but Christian homeland they could see a land of light beyond a wide river. One day, while tending their flocks, they had heard the enchanting, sweet sound of bells, such as those of the great abbey of St. Edmund, and after long wanderings they had found themselves entering the bright sunshine of the cornfields of Woolpit. So great was the warmth and power of the sun to them that they nearly fainted and they had been anxiously and dazedly trying to find the entrance to the cave from which they emerged when they had been discovered by strange people whose skin was not green.

Eight miles westward of Woolpit and not far from the ruins of St. Edmund's abbey are the three Fornhams - St. Genevieve, All Saints and St. Martin. They lie close to the banks of the River Lark with Fornham St. Martin not two miles from the abbey founded by Sigebert, seventh century king who became a monk. But perhaps significantly as far as the tale of the two green children of Woolpit is concerned,

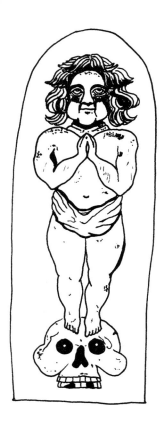
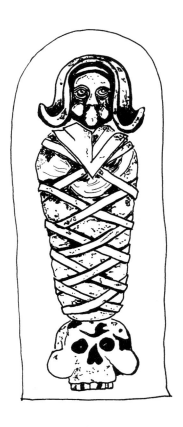

ABOVE - *Thomas Shute aged 9 who died in 1669 a few months after his sister Ann who was 'borne & dide' the same May day. She is shown wrapped in chrysom cloth.*

Fornham St. Martin is north of the Lark and the abbey is to the south of it. Could it be that the youngsters were children of pauper parents living off a monotonous diet of beans and berries in a wretched, woodland hovel? One day, in a prankish mood for adventure, the girl, who is described in the chronicle as skittish and headstrong, may have led her young brother towards the sound of bells coming from the land of light where even at night candles and tapers shone in the darkness. Their meanderings led them across Rougham heath and with nightfall the tree-lined paths must have seemed cavernous and endless as they desperately sought a way home. Next day they were found disorientated by fatigue, hunger and fear. Surrounded by staring strangers, their speech delivered amid bouts of inconsolable weeping may well have been incomprehensible. From the accounts it seems that once the initial shock had passed, they learned the language remarkably quickly. And is it any wonder that a strong-willed girl should wish to exchange the drudgery of serfdom for the life of a servant in a rich man's house?

The tale of another young brother and sister whose grim fate was to die in each other's arms amid the terrors of the forest is better known because every year their story is parodied in pantomime - they were the 'Babes in the Wood'.

> *These pretty babes, with hand in hand,*
> *Went wandering up and downe;*
> *But never more could see the man*
> *Approaching from the town;*
> *Their pretty lippes with black-berries*
> *Were all besmeared and dyed;*
> *And when they sawe the darksome night,*
> *They sat them downe and cryed.*

Their tale was told in an Elizabethan ballad, and tradition places the scene of the tragedy in Wayland or Wailing Wood between Watton and Griston. On his deathbed, the babes' father had placed them in the care of his brother, their 'wicked uncle', who was tempted to make the children's inheritance his own. The uncle paid two villains to take the children into the woods and murder them, but one of the hired killers had a change of heart and killed his accomplice who had been determined to carry out the evil contract. The frightened and bewildered young children were then abandoned deep in the forest where they wandered vainly seeking a path to safety. Eventually the two weeping innocents, exhausted and hungry, sat beneath a tree until, holding each other in their arms, death ended their ordeal and the birds of the forest covered their bodies with leaves.

> *Thus wandered these poor innocents*
> *Till death did end their grief,*
> *In one another's arms they dyed,*
> *As wanting due relief;*
> *No burial this pretty pair*
> *Of any man receives,*
> *Till Robin Redbreast piously*
> *Did cover them with leaves.*

The wicked uncle, however, did not profit from his conspiracy. Misfortune dogged him - his barns burned down, his cattle died of disease and his sons drowned before he himself died in jail, broken and deep in debt. The spirits of the young brother and sister, it is said, still wander through the Wailing Wood and, sometimes, their piteous cries can be heard in the 'darksome night'.

No stone marks the graves of these boys and girls but real tragedies are recalled by memorials in many East Anglian churches and graveyards. Some bear grinning, eyeless skulls with a few words of caution for the beholder, and others carry elaborate, cherubic carvings with elegiac inscriptions compiled by grieving parents.

A series of 17th century memorials set into the floor of the quiet, little church at Heckingham display a series of skulls with the old warnings *HODIE MIHI CRAS TIBI (Me today, you tomorrow) and Tempas fuget, memento mei, mors venet (Time passes, remember me, death comes)*. These slabs recall the Crowe family among whom several children died in childhood when the rate of infant mortality was very high and, as some memorials state, 'physicians were in vain'. Sometimes the implied criticism of doctors was somewhat harsh as in the case of Edmond Skepper of Beccles who died in 1771 - *A lingring sickness did me seize of which no Physicians could me ease.* He was 81 years old. In some cases the cause of premature death is woven into the verses of the epitaph to warn others to be more careful.

> *I drove a team the horse was young,*
> *To manage him I tried,*
> *A bramble cross'd my path, I fell,*
> *The wheels they prest my side.*

This memorial in Ashby churchyard recalls a young victim of a wagon accident and a similar one is at Caston. Above the porch of Colney church is a stone to John Fox aged 79, a man of humble station, *a worthy and useful Member of society, an honest and industrious Labourer* who was trampled by a team of horses. The memorial to this experienced wagoner concludes - *READER, If thou drivest a team be careful & endanger not the life of another or thine own.* As another stone at Colney says –

> *Life hangs upon a slender thread*
> *Which soon is snapt and we are dead,*
> *In health at noon, at evening gone...*

Set into the wall of Haddiscoe churchyard is a stone in memory of Will Salter, a stagecoach man who died in 1776. He was *Always punctual, always just, his horses cou'd they speak wou'd tell they lov'd their good old master well. He had one journey left, Elija like drive up to heaven, take the reward of all his pains and leave to other hands the reins.* At Coston a stone marks the untimely loss of a lad struck by a windmill sail. At Beccles a headstone tells of a boy drowned in the river, *short was the time he left his home, No more alive for to return,* and at Great Yarmouth another young victim of drowning after the collapse of a bridge is remembered by a headstone on which is carved the scene of bridge and people falling into the river. Occasionally a headstone is to be found marking the grave of a victim of 'foul play' as in the churchyard of Holy Trinity, Bungay, where a young man *cruelly murdered* lies buried. Henry Scarle, who *was Valued when alive and Regretted now Dead* was killed by robbers in 1787. The indignation of the law-abiding community was made plain on his stone - *Honest industrious Men were never known to Commit such a Horrid Outrage as this.* Such a phrase might have been the epitaph of those trusting but treacherously abandoned babes of Wayland Wood, two *lovely buds, so young & fair cut off by early doom, just came to show how sweet the flowers in paradise will bloom.*

For many centuries, whether by accident, neglect or illness, death was an accepted and expected feature of family life. It was normal for a quarter to a third of children to die before they reached 15 years and this high rate of mortality did not decline until the mid-18th century. Pictures in stone or brass of babes and children who died in their early years are to be seen in many churches, some wrapped in their chrysom robes, some helpless in tightly drawn swaddling bands. St. Mary's church, Rougham, in Norfolk has some of the finest brasses in the county including one showing two infants, John and Roger Yelverton, who died in 1505 and 1510, bound in their chrysom sheets. New-born babes were clothed in the chrysom garment for baptism and continued to wear it for a month until the mother had been 'churched' by the priest in a rite of purification and blessing. Should the chrysom child die during that period it was buried in the garment.

At Huntingfield, where, in the 19th century, the rector's wife spent years painting golden-winged angels, saints and texts on the roof, another priest placed a memorial slab carved with the likenesses of *the Sole issue of their mournfull Parents* near the altar. The two children, a boy of 9 effusively described as *an exceeding Beautiful, Apprehensive, Ingenuous & Hopefull Child* is shown with innocent face while his sister, who was born and died on the same day, is depicted as a 'chrysom babe'. To emphasise their transient mortality each stands upon a skull.

ABOVE - *young David Birde, son of the rector, shown sleeping in his cot on a brass at Boxford. He died in 1606. Note his little shoes poking out under the bed.*

Wild and Wicked Men, Children Green and Tragic

During the 19th century, under pressure from Church authorities, the amusing and quaintly concocted headstone verses gave way to a line or phrase of biblical text. Churchyard doggerel disappeared and there were no more warnings such as *Death with his dart did pierce my heart in the middle of my prime,* or, like that to a Dunwich teenager -

> *When I left home I little thought my glass so near was run,*
> *But Death! alas did call on me, and lo! my work was done.*

Many brasses and memorials show that some families had no difficulty producing heirs, as in the case of Richard Calthorpe who died in 1562. His brass in St. Mary's church, Antingham, which shares a churchyard with the ruined St. Margaret's, shows him with his 19 children - 14 sons and five daughters. Another large family of Calthorpes is remembered at Cockthorpe where Sir John and his wife had 14 children by whom *the auncient glory of the name and family did reflorish and is dilatated into many of the best houses in this country.* Before she died in 1639 aged 86, Dame Barbara *was much comforted with the sight of 193 of her children and their offspring.* At Holme-next-the-Sea where the Peddars Way reaches the coast, a memorial to Richard and Clemens Stone, says they were married for 64 years, had 13 children and 72 grandchildren whom the grandparents *to their greate comforte did behoulde.* John Browne of Halesworth *lyved a quyet lyfe* and died in 1581 aged 80 years and 25 weeks. *He hadd bye his onely wiffe, with whom he lyved fifty four yeares and ffive monethes, six sons, and ten daughters. He hadd also 65 Grandchildren of whom 54 were livinge at the daye of his decease.* The brass inscription and the pictures of John's wife and 16 children were found in the Waveney in 1825 but John's likeness is lost.

Monks and Monasteries Saints and Skulls

East Anglian legends have preserved many tales of ghostly monks haunting the old, ivy-clad ruins of abbeys and priories. In the centuries before King Henry VIII closed the monasteries and confiscated their treasure and lands, monks, nuns and friars had been a familiar part of life. Large towns like Norwich, Cambridge and Ipswich had several monasteries and friaries and at Bury St. Edmunds, Ely and St. Benet's abbey near Ludham there were great Benedictine monasteries of ancient foundation.

Bury St. Edmunds commemorates East Anglia's martyr-king and its abbey was among the biggest, richest and most famous in Europe. It guarded St. Edmund's shrine where the barons gathered in opposition to cruel King John on the saint's feast day in 1214, an act which led to the granting of Magna Carta. The abbey is now a ruin but the 12th century Norman Tower and later abbey gatehouse remain, as do the medieval churches of St. James, now the diocesan cathedral, and St. Mary. Between the two churches were the abbey cemetery and charnel house where a less substantial reminder of the monastic past might be seen - the restless ghost of a monk in a black habit, his cowl hiding a faceless head as he silently patrols the abbey precincts. Houses were built into the wall of the huge abbey church and close by is a modern statue of St. Edmund and a memorial to 17 other martyrs, some farm workers and weavers, burned in the saint's town for their beliefs. On the wall of the charnel house ruins, where the bones of the dead were stored, a stone urges passers-by to reflect on the fate of a servant girl hanged for opening the door of her employer's home to her burglar lover. *Reader, pause at this humble stone, it records the fate of unguarded youth by the allurements of vice and the treacherous snares of seduction. Sarah Lloyd on the 23rd of April, 1800 in the*

22nd year of her age, suffered a just but ignominious death for admitting her abandoned seducer into the dwelling house of her mistress in the night of 3d Oct 1799 and becoming the instrument in his hands of the crimes of robbery and house-burning. These were her last words: May my example be a warning to thousands.

Another stone on the old charnel house is a reminder of another tragedy - Mary Haselton, only nine years old, struck by lightning while saying her prayers in 1785. Her chilling epitaph tells -

> *For whilst the Thunder's awful voice was heard*
> *The little suppliant with its hands uprear'd*
> *Addressed her God in prayers the Priest had taught,*
> *His mercy crav'd, and his protection sought.*
> *Learn Reader hence, that Wisdom to adore*
> *Thou can'st not scan: & fear his boundless Power*
> *Safe shalt thou be, if thou perform'st his will*
> *Blest if he spares, and more blest should he kill.*

A few miles away in Hessett church, among the wall paintings, is St. Barbara, the protector against thunder - storms and the patroness of gunners and fire fighters.

The defeat and murder of Edmund, last of the Saxon kings of East Anglia, by the invading heathen Danes in November 869 resulted in many legendary tales and it is ironic that his subsequent popularity as a national hero-saint owes much to a Dane who became king of England. The action of Cnut, the king who is said to have vainly commanded the tide to retreat to expose the flattery of his courtiers, in encouraging the cult of a long dead East Anglian king appears strange had he known the tale of how his father, Sweyn Forkbeard, king of England for a few months, was killed in the midst of his soldiers by the saint's invisible ghost. If Cnut did know of the tale, he must have decided that the political value of the cult of East Anglia's martyr-king should override any filial duty to his pagan father's memory.

Edmund was 14 when he became king and at once the miracles associated with his name began. Tradition says he survived a shipwreck on his way to his new realm and that when he came safely ashore at St. Edmund's Point near Hunstanton a spring of healing water burst forth as he knelt to pray. He was crowned on Christmas Day 855 at Bures on a site marked by an early 13th century chapel which now houses three armed effigies of de Vere Earls of Oxford. In the year that Edmund received his crown the heathen Danes wintered in England for the first time instead of going home with their loot - it was an ominous sign that the fair weather raids were to become a campaign of conquest.

Legend says that the pious king's downfall resulted from the jealousy of one of his companions. It is a tale of murder and revenge in which the characters were real enough but the story is a concoction, probably designed to enhance the king's saintly reputation and attribute his defeat and martyrdom to the treachery of a man he thought a friend. The story is that a Danish nobleman, Ragnar Lothbrog, was hunting one day when suddenly a storm blew up which carried him and his small boat out to sea. For days he drifted westward until he made landfall in the estuary of the River Yare at Reedham. He was taken to the young king's court and made welcome. Soon he showed his talent for hunting which aroused the jealousy of Beorn, the king's huntsman. Angered by the favour the king showed Ragnar, Beorn lured the Dane into the woods, killed him and buried the body but Edmund became suspicious at the sudden disappearance of his guest. Ragnar's faithful hunting dog led them to the grave and the crime was discovered. Beorn was set adrift in the boat which had brought Ragnar to England and by chance the winds and tides carried him across the North Sea to Denmark where he told his victim's sons, Ingware and Ubba, that Edmund had ordered their father to be put to death. The brothers raised a great army of Vikings and set sail in a fleet of longships to seek revenge. At Barnby on the Suffolk bank of the Waveney there is a tradition that Edmund gained a victory over the Danes when he surprised them as they landed in the marshes.

ABOVE - *the 12th century Norman Tower, once the main gateway to the great abbey at Bury St. Edmunds. It was at the martyred king's shrine that the barons gathered in 1214 to pledge their opposition to King John. A few months later the monarch was forced by an army, led by Robert Fitzwalter, to put his seal to Magna Carta. Among the clauses of the great charter it was laid down that widows should not be forced to marry and no one should be arrested for murder on the evidence of a woman unless the victim was her husband. Baron Fitzwalter, Lord of Dunmow, is the man said to have started the custom of giving a flitch of bacon to a happily married couple. In the foreground is a modern statue of St. Edmund.*

The issue was settled when Edmund met them in battle near Thetford where his outnumbered army of East Anglians was overwhelmed. The defeated monarch fled but was betrayed to the Danes who offered to spare his life if he would renounce his Christian faith and be their vassal. Edmund refused so he was tied to a tree, shot with arrows and beheaded.

Hoxne in Suffolk is the traditional site of Edmund's betrayal and death, and a bridge in the village is said to bear the saint's curse. As Edmund fled from his enemies he hid beneath Goldbrook Bridge but the glinting reflection of his golden spurs was seen in the water by a bride and bridegroom as they made their way home from their wedding. Once more the betrayal theme is woven into the legend as the newly-weds told the Danes of the king's hiding place. As he was led away Edmund cried his curse on any bridal couple who crossed the bridge on their wedding day.

ABOVE - *Goldbrook Bridge at Hoxne where legend says that King Edmund was hiding when he was betrayed to the Danes by two newly-weds. In revenge he put a curse on the bridge.*

When the Danes departed some of the king's men returned to claim his body which they found still tied to the tree but there was no trace of his head. For several days their search was in vain until a voice was heard among the trees crying 'Here, here, here!' Guided by the sound, the searchers found the king's head lying between the front paws of a guardian wolf. The martyred king was buried at Sutton close to the Suffolk coast and a small wooden chapel built to his memory. Early in the 10th century Edmund's body was removed to a new shrine at Bury St. Edmunds but another Danish invasion of East Anglia in 1010 caused its hasty removal to London. Sweyn Forkbeard, Cnut's father, is said to have met his end when he threatened to burn the saint's shrine and torture the monks of Bury St. Edmunds unless he was paid a tribute of gold. In February 1014, as he made merry at a banquet surrounded by Danish warriors, the spectre of St. Edmund appeared but only Sweyn could see the spirit armed with a spear as it marched avengingly towards him. The Dane screamed in terror as the spectre, invisible to all those around him, plunged the spear into his body. After hours of agony the heathen marauder went to his Valhalla.

A stone church was built on Cnut's orders to shelter the saint's grave at Bury St. Edmunds and Benedictine monks from the abbeys at St. Benet's Hulme and Ely were drafted in to administer the shrine. Cnut and Edward the Confessor endowed the abbey with lands and privileges and soon the shrine of the martyr-king became a goal for pilgrims. The Normans replaced Cnut's church with a much grander one. Protected by walls and towers it grew to be one of the finest abbey precincts in Christendom. The defences were necessary because as at Norwich and Cambridge, relations between monks and townspeople were occasionally quarrelsome and violent. The people of Bury pulled down the abbey gate in 1327 and the present one is the one they had to build in reparation. The abbey was stormed again during the Peasants Revolt. The collapse of towers and fires punctuated the history of the monastery until its dissolution in 1538. In 1198 Abbot Sampson and a select group of monks entered the saint's shrine and when the tomb was opened they found the head and body united and uncorrupted. What became of Edmund's body no one knows. One tale says it was carried off by defeated French troops in 1217 but the bones of the holy royal hero, once venerated by kings, probably lie near the ruined abbey church *dead now, and dumb; but was alive once, and spake.*

ABOVE - *the legendary story of the wolf guarding the martyred King Edmund's head is depicted in a carving at Walpole St Peter church.*

Edmund was the most illustrious of the Saxon royal saints of East Anglia and his importance is reflected by the many representations of him in church art across the region. He is shown on the Thornham Parva retable holding an arrow, the symbol of his martyrdom, and among the many screen pictures of him are those at Ranworth, Ludham, Barton Turf, Somerleyton and Kersey. A painting of Edmund is on a pier in St. Mary's, Lakenheath, and on the chancel wall of the thatched and round-towered Norman church dedicated to him at Fritton, Suffolk, is a picture executed more than eight centuries ago showing Danish archers aiming their bows. Carvings of a wolf holding the saint's head between its paws are in St. Mary's, Hadleigh, and Walpole St. Peter. Another royal East Anglian revered as a martyr and saint was Ethelbert, treacherously murdered in 794 by his host, Offa, when he sought marriage with that Mercian king's daughter.

Ely had the shrines of several royal East Anglian saints. Etheldreda, daughter of King Anna, was founder-abbess and was followed in turn by her sister Sexburga and niece Ermenilda. Etheldreda's other sainted sisters were Ethelburga, an abbess in France, and Withburga whose well of healing water is in the churchyard at East Dereham. Withburga's body was stolen one night by the abbot and monks of Ely after they had wined and dined the men of Dereham. Hurrying away with their sacred cargo, the monks eluded their furious pursuers by taking boat at Brandon and rowing as fast as they could along the network of Fenland rivers to the safety of their island monastery. St. Withburga's symbol is a white doe that is said to have sustained her with its milk during her time as a religious solitary. Withburga with her doe and holding a church is portrayed with Edmund and Etheldreda on the screen at Barnham Broom. The sisters are also on the damaged screen at Burlingham St. Andrew and at Oxborough where the steeple fell in 1948. Other representations of Etheldreda, the austere, twice-wed virgin, are in Ely Cathedral where incidents from her life, including the miracles which attended her escape from her second husband who sought to take her to his bed, are carved high on the stone pillars of the octagon. At Blythburgh the carved chancel frontals of apostles and saints include two which are said to be Etheldreda and Anna, her father-king. Nine centuries ago the manor of Willingham was bequeathed to God and St. Etheldreda so perhaps a female figure near a lancet window of the church is the oldest surviving picture of the saint whose name was unworthily corrupted via St. Audrey to tawdry to indicate something cheap and nasty. The blame for that lies with medieval profiteers who sold gaudy but inferior wares at St. Audrey's fair. St. Etheldreda in the guise of her alias St. Audrey is among a curious selection of saints on the screen of Gateley church which includes Louis the crusader king of France, John Shorne with a devil peering disconsolately out of a boot, and uniquely 'Sancta Puella Ridibowne' which may be an alias of St. Christina of Redburne. These saints and that sometimes demented monarch Henry VI, founder of Eton and King's College, Cambridge, who is also on the Gateley screen, are curious companions for the Holy Virgin and St. Augustine. Was murdered Henry, the pious but uncanonised patron of learning, included at Ludham, Barton Turf, Nayland and Eye to show support for his cult or that local sympathy had been with the Lancastrians (Tudors) during the Wars of the Roses?

Five years before William the Bastard, Duke of Normandy, led his army of tough adventurers across the English Channel to conquer Harold's kingdom, Richeldis de Faverches, the devout lady of Walsingham Parva manor, had a vision in which she was instructed to build a replica of the house in Nazareth where the Virgin Mary had been told by an angel that she was to be the mother of the Messiah. So began the legendary stories associated with the picturesque Norfolk village that became the home of England's most famous shrine. Soon kings and commoners, rich nobles and paupers were making pilgrimages to the shrine of Our Lady of Walsingham.

ABOVE - *the shrine of Our Lady of Walsingham. The church was built in the 1930's and is claimed to be the original site of the Holy House*

The first problem for Richeldis had been where to site her replica house. In the field where she had had the vision two plots remained dry after heavy overnight dew and taking this as a sign she decided to build on the site nearest two springs but soon things went wrong. No matter how hard they tried the builders could not get the timbers to fit together square and true. Richeldis spent the night praying and the next day the ramshackle construction had become perfect but on the other site. In the 12th century Richeldis's son founded an Augustinian Priory whose monks administered England's Nazareth and the wooden house was moved close to the Priory church and given the shelter of a chapel. The red brick church built in the 1930s to house the modern shrine is said to be on the original, miraculously indicated site with its Saxon holy well found during the building work.

With the passage of time an effigy of the Virgin and Child superseded the little wooden house as the main object of veneration. Relics shown to pilgrims included what was claimed to be one of St. Peter's finger joints and a crystal phial of the Virgin's milk. Miraculous cures of the lame, blind and leprous were claimed as well as relief from the vexation of wicked spirits. Once a fleeing mounted knight was said to have been transported to the sanctuary of the shrine when he invoked the Virgin. The infuriated pursuer who had been on the point of catching his prey was left outside to wonder how horse and rider could pass through a gate so small. Stories that the shrine was really the original holy house flown to Norfolk by angels and that the Virgin Mother had removed herself to the shrine by the River Stiffkey because the Saracens ruled the Holy Land attracted even more pilgrims to Walsingham in search of her blessing or cure. Along the routes to Walsingham chapels were built and the closest to the shrine was the Slipper Chapel at Houghton St. Giles where pilgrims removed their shoes to walk the last mile and a half barefoot. Henry VIII walked shoeless for two miles to the shrine from East Barsham Manor before politics and greed led him to order the end of Walsingham's Holy House and Priory in 1538. The sacred effigy of Our Lady of Walsingham was carried to London to join the images of other pilgrimage cults on a bonfire. The previous year Nicholas Mileham, the Sub Prior, and others had been found guilty of plotting treason - some were only voicing their fear that the policy of monastic closures was threatening their livelihood - and barbaric executions of hanging, drawing and quartering followed on Walsingham's Martyrs' Field.

> *Weepe, weepe, O Walsingham whose dayes are nightes,*
> *Blessings turned to blasphemies, holy deedes to dispites.*
> *Sinne is wher Our Ladie sat, heaven turned is to hell,*
> *Satan sittes wher Our Lord did swaye, Walsingham, oh farewell.*

Walsingham's 400 years without pilgrims were ended by Father Alfred Hope Patten who was appointed vicar in 1921. He immediately began planning the restoration of the shrine for 20th century pilgrims and his endeavour proved successful and once more Walsingham thrives on the pilgrim trade. There has been no such reversal of fortune for another north Norfolk priory which achieved fame almost overnight thanks to a deal agreed between its prior and a wandering hawker of relics in 1223. William Langland wrote his 'Vision of Piers the Plowman' towards the end of the 14th century and in it he makes the cheat Avarice vow to end his swindling tricks and go with his crafty wife on a pilgrimage to Walsingham and then to pray to the Holy Roode of Bromholm to be delivered from his debts. It was an old piece of wood that suddenly sent a poor and out-of-the-way monastery rocketing up the league table of most popular shrines.

The small Cluniac priory of Bromholm had been founded in 1113 by the lord of the manor on the exposed North Sea coast at Bacton. But it was not until that shrewd or inspired piece of speculation was concluded 110 years later that Bromholm, and its Holy Roode caught the imagination of pilgrims. The relic had belonged to Baldwin, Count of

Flanders and Emperor of Constantinople, who carried it with him into battle to ensure victory. But one day he neglected to do so and was defeated and killed by the infidels and on receiving news of the disaster, the chaplain scooped up as many relics and jewels as he could and set sail for England where he touted his holy antiques around the monasteries. He sold some jewels and two of St. Margaret's fingers but none of the suspicious monks would purchase his little cross said to have been made from the wood of the True Cross. Eventually he came to Bromholm where the prior and brother monks accepted his tale and they agreed to take the relic as well as him and his two sons into their care. Tales soon spread of the efficacy of Bromholm's Holy Roode - many had been raised from the dead, the sightless and the crippled cured, and devils cast out. Henry III, a frequent visitor to Walsingham, endowed the priory with privileges and Bromholm prospered until it was closed three centuries later.

Monks and Monastries, Saints and Skulls

East Anglia also had many shrines to saints of local renown. Thorney Abbey held the relics of Huna, a 7th century Fenland hermit, and of a trio of hermits slain by the Danes who had defeated Edmund. The same Danes sacked Peterborough, killed Abbot Hedda and his monks and left the abbey a ruin for a century. Fenland's most famous saint was Guthlac of Crowland who become a hermit on a demon-infested isle in the fens. After suffering the torments of these ugly devils he chased them into the sea with a whip and his reputation attracted others to lead a life of isolation. A gift of *fenne fyshe* to Thomas Cromwell from Crowland's abbot failed to save the abbey and shrine from dissolution in 1539, but a statue of Guthlac with a whip and a fiend at his feet still stands among those of apostles, kings and abbots on the abbey ruins.

A cult which appealed to the men who tilled and toiled on the land of medieval Norfolk was that centred on the church at Bawburgh, a village which straddles the River Yare four miles west of the old heart of Norwich. The legend of Walstan, the royal prince who lived the life of a poor ploughman, proved enduringly attractive to the farm labourers whose lives were governed by the seasons. Walstan was said to have given up the privileges of royal birth and entered the service of a farmer at Taverham. He gave his food and shoes to the poor and when his employer's wife went to rebuke him for his uncommon charity, she found him working barefoot and unhurt amid the thorns. The farmer offered to make Walstan his heir but this was rejected and Walstan asked only for a calf soon to be born on the farm. Two bull calves were born and they were carefully reared and tended by the saint who had been told by an angel that they would bear his body to his grave site. Later the angel appeared again as Walstan laboured in the fields and warned him of the time of his death. As the hour approached he prayed that any farm

LEFT - *Bawburgh Church was once the site of the shrine of St. Walstan to which Norfolk farmers came seeking the saint's blessing on their animals.*

worker who came to his grave should be cured of sickness and his stock freed of murrain. At the moment of death a white dove flew from his mouth and then his body was placed upon a cart and the two oxen allowed to wander because only they knew where Walstan was to lie.

Walstan's oxen plodded south, crossing the Wensum as if its waters were stone, before pausing on a hill where a spring of cool water burst forth. The saint's strange hearse crossed the Tud and Yare until it reached Bawburgh where another spring appeared. The church, now with red-tiled roof and capped round tower, was built on the site but the shrine chapel has gone. Bawburgh's cult of St. Walstan was important only in Norfolk but the offerings of husbandmen seeking the saint's blessing for themselves and their animals were such that six chantry priests recited masses at his shrine. Walstan is shown with two oxen on Barnham Broom's screen and with a scythe at Ludham. He is also shown at Burlingham St. Andrew and Sparham.

Standing gaunt against the Broadland sky on the finger of marshland formed by the rivers Ant, Bure and Thurne are the ruins of the once powerful abbey of St. Benet's. The brick tower of a long abandoned windmill rears upward amid the fragments of ruined walls which once protected the Benedictine monks. The monastery was attacked in 1381 during the Peasants Revolt but it is the tale of an earlier siege and double treachery which has been preserved by the long memory of folklore. Cnut the Dane had favoured the isolated abbey which grew wealthy and powerful with land in dozens of Norfolk villages. A generation later the ruthless Normans, the descendants of earlier armies of Norse predators, spread across the land in search of the spoils of conquest. In the marshes beside the Bure, as in the fens around Ely, King William's men were met with fierce and determined opposition. The monks could sleep safe in their beds while the impatient and frustrated invaders floundered in the marshy mud. Inside the abbey, however, one of the brethren had ambitions contrary to his vow of obedience - he aspired to rule as abbot. One night he slipped into the darkness outside the walls and hurried along safe and familiar paths to the enemy encampment.

ABOVE - *the Broadland ruins of St. Benet's Abbey gatehouse are dominated by the tower of an 18th century mill. The abbey near Ludham escaped dissolution, being united with the Norwich bishopric, but the buildings were abandoned about 450 years ago.*

A pact of betrayal was agreed. The gates would be opened and the monk rewarded with the mitre. The next evening the Normans stealthily gathered unseen in the gloom and when their trusting ally unbarred the gate they gave a great shout and stormed inside. Opposition was quickly quelled and the monks soon rounded up to be told that their abbey dedicated to St. Benedict on the banks of the Bure had a new abbot. The perfidious brother stepped forward, his ambition satisfied as the victors placed the cope over his shoulders and the mitre on his head. He smiled a smile of self-satisfaction as the symbols of abbacial authority were placed into his hands. The rough, brutish Normans had honoured their pledge! But that smile vanished from his face when the same coarse warrior hands suddenly lifted him off his feet and bundled him to the abbey gateway. A noose was thrust around his neck and the brief reign of the new abbot ended as he was jerked into oblivion. The smiling Normans knew how best to reward a traitor. Some nights, they say, a shadowy figure of a wailing, wriggling monk can be seen when the moon casts a silver gloss on the waters of the Bure.

The spirit of another monk, a man whose gentle talent and character was unsullied by aspirations of temporal advancement, is said to silently haunt the waterways of Broadland near Ranworth. His only companion, as he glides inaudibly among the reeds, is a dog seated in the prow of the spectral boat. As the threatening storm clouds of closure gathered around England's monasteries, one of the Benedictine brothers of St. Benet's abbey would depart each morning and row the two miles to St. Helen's church at Ranworth. On a good summer day one can see the villages of Broadland from Norwich to the coast from the church tower. Week after week the monk in black cowl and habit, and his dog made the dawn journey to Ranworth where, with the delicate touch and precise eye on an artist, he skilfully refurbished the rood screen. At evening, when the sun began to sink in the sky beyond the slender spire of Norwich cathedral, the monk returned to his boat at the staithe to be greeted by his patient dog and return to his cell in the abbey.

One evening the brother who could create beauty to the glory of God came back to his monastery home to find it empty and silent. No chant came from the abbey church. No bell tolled the call to evensong. Nobody disturbed the dusky stillness of the cloister. The king's men had been to St. Benet's. East Anglia's oldest monastery governed by the Rule of St. Benedict was an empty shell invaded only by the murmur of the reeds swaying in the wind. The gentle monk with pain and despair in his heart never came again to Ranworth, at least not in life this side of the grave. Sometimes, they say, a small boat with a dog in it may be seen moored close to the church and that is a sign that an ephemeral monkish figure is kneeling in prayer before Ranworth's glorious rood screen. Ranworth's screen is among the finest in the land, its painted panels depicting apostles and saints. Another treasure of the church is the illuminated manuscript Antiphoner on sheep hide, the work of monks of Langley Abbey in 1400.

Many centuries ago other Benedictine monks had to shelter behind the walls of Binham Priory when an ally of their deposed prior sought the reinstatement of his friend by force of arms. Robert Fitzwalter, lord of Dunmow, attacked when his comrade prior was sent packing. The siege was raised by King John who angrily exclaimed, *'By God's feet, I or Fitzwalter must be king of England!'* He despatched troops to separate the warring parties. North Norfolk was dotted with monastic houses with other priories at Flitcham, Weybourne, Docking and Beeston Regis, an abbey at North Creake and friaries at Blakeney and Burnham Norton. Some may have been attracted to the area by Walsingham's fame, and legend says that Binham had a secret underground passage to England's Nazareth. The tale is that one day a curious fiddler and his dog entered the mysterious tunnel playing on his violin so that his progress could be tracked by his companions. Stooping to hear the fiddler's subterranean music, they wandered across the fields towards Walsingham three miles away until, suddenly, the music ceased. They hastened back to the entrance to find the lost fiddler's dog but no sign of the musician. Had the intrepid musician encountered the ghost of a black-robed monk that is reputed to haunt the secret passage? An identical tale is told of another fiddler who disappeared while exploring a tunnel which led to the remains of Anstey's Norman castle near Royston. Again, only the dog was ever seen again.

ABOVE - *the remains of Binham's Benedictine Priory which legend claims has a secret tunnel to Walsingham. Part of the dissolved monastery became the parish church.*

The little Suffolk town of Clare has much to entice those wishing to seek out the past. A rarity indeed for East Anglia is its pre-Roman hillfort, and there are the ruins of a Norman castle, a 15th century richly pargeted priest's house, the old Swan Inn and large medieval church with a 1790 sundial above the porch telling churchyard idlers to *Go about your business.* It was in the church that the grim-faced Puritan William Dowsing, attired in sombre garb and tall hat, passed his busiest day of destruction in 1643 by smashing 1,000 'superstitious pictures' and pulling down carvings of saints and cherubim. How the godly folk of Clare must have cursed Parliament's vandal when he left them without their windows of glowing painted glass to keep out the January wind.

Clare also has its priory where, so legend tells, Hugh the sacristan lost his soul to the Devil five hundred years ago. This house of Austin Friars had been established in 1248 by Richard de Clare, the powerful Earl of Gloucester and Hertford, and under that family's patronage the friars of Clare grew in wealth and influence. But by the 15th century when the legendary events are said to have occurred, discipline had become slack and regard for the Rule of St. Augustine of Hippo was neglected.

Presiding over this lax regime was Galfridus, the Prior of Clare, whose worldly ways did not inspire abstinence and self-denial. Hugh had charge of the valuables and foolishly he had raised money to indulge his fancies by borrowing heavily and pawning treasures in his care. Concerned at his predicament and fearing that an inspection might reveal his misuse of priory assets, Hugh wandered along the banks of the Stour desperately trying to think of a remedy. Here he met a stranger wearing a monk's habit who was surprisingly sympathetic and, better still, suggested a simple scheme to end the sacristan's worries. Those candles which he sold to pious folk to burn in the church, could they not be put out, trimmed and sold again? The stranger added a warning that the first candle saved should be set aside and if it should be used, then the moment its flame died Hugh's soul would be

71

forfeit. Hugh set aside the first candle as instructed and as the months passed his fears gradually eased until the fateful day an errand led him to enter the priory cellars. Thinking he would be but a few moments he lit the stranger's candle and set it down as he surveyed the shelves of food. Hugh compounded his folly by allowing thoughts of how best to fill his belly to drive caution from his mind and when he returned up the cellar steps the candle was left to burn lower and lower. That night the neglected, flickering flame spluttered and died, and as it did so the corridors of the priory echoed with a terrifying scream. When the friars found Hugh's horribly twisted and bloody body, its flesh was singed and burned, and there was the odour of sulphur in the air!

Two miles downstream from Clare is Cavendish, its village green lined by thatched cottages behind which rises the church tower with a room with a fireplace to comfort the sacristan in winter. In 1381, when the Peasants' Revolt exploded in Suffolk and John Wrawe, a 'scandalous' priest from Ringsfield, led his mob against Bury's great abbey, Sir John Cavendish, Chief Justice of England, hastened to secure his valuables in the tower belfry - the word then meant a secure place. He then fled but the rebels caught up with him at Lakenheath and chopped off his head. The Prior of Bury suffered the same fate and in London that day, Simon of Sudbury, Archbishop of Canterbury and the king's Chancellor, was dragged from the Tower and decapitated. The archbishop's head was put up on London Bridge until it was replaced by the head of Wat Tyler, the man who had led the revolt. Simon's skull was sent to rest in St. Gregory's church in his home town and Cavendish church gained a new chancel as a result of Sir John's will which was enacted sooner that he might have hoped.

The headless bones of Brythnoth, the Saxon hero killed by Vikings a thousand years ago, rest at Ely. The giant earl's bones were found in the cathedral in 1770 but his skull is probably in the mud of the Blackwater near Maldon where he fought his last battle.

Monks and Monastries, Saints and Skulls

A famous skull which found rest in Sidney Sussex College, Cambridge, after three centuries was that of Lord Protector Oliver Cromwell. When Charles II gained the throne in 1660, the regicide's embalmed body was dug up and dragged to Tyburn where the head was chopped off. Impaled on Westminster Hall, the skull blew down in a gale and passed through various hands until it was buried in a secret spot near the college chapel in 1960. Ironically, Cromwell's college, built on the site of a Franciscan friary, had been so staunchly Royalist during the Civil War that its former student's soldiers had thrown the Master and Fellows into the street.

Fame and Fortune, Rags to Riches

Fame and fortune, or at least the latter, have been and still are the dream of thousands of people. For the majority it must remain an unfulfilled fantasy - how many dreams are shattered each week by the wrong numbers on their lottery ticket. But one man who, so legend says, followed his dream and was rewarded beyond expectation was John Chapman of Swaffham. He was no mythical man and certainly he was wealthy because his money helped to pay for the rebuilding of the town's church. It was the manner in which he acquired his wealth that became the stuff of legend.

John, so the tale runs, was a pedlar who, with his wife, earned a modest living by selling his wares from a market stall. One night he had a strange dream telling him that if he went to London he would meet a man who would give him some good news. John could not get the haunting dream out of his mind so, after several restless nights, he set out on the 100 mile journey to the capital where he walked up and down on London Bridge waiting to be accosted by an unknown messenger. After some hours a shopkeeper who had noticed the loitering pedlar approached John and asked him what he was doing. John told him of the curious dream and his apparently wasted journey. *'Alas, good friend,' replied the shopkeeper, 'if I heeded dreams I might have proved myself as much a fool as thou. Not long since I dreamt that at a town called Swaffham Market, in Norfolk, dwells one John Chapman, a pedlar, who hath a tree at the back of his house under which is buried a pot of money. If I had made the journey thither to dig for hidden treasure on account of a dream would I not have been mocked as a fool?'*

John smiled, promised he would obey no more foolish dreams and then hurried back to Swaffham where he rushed into his garden with a spade and began digging. He was soon rewarded by the discovery of a pot of money, on the lid of which were some words of Latin. Pedlar John was no scholar but he was cunning. He displayed the inscription in his window and waited for a learned passer-by to decipher the ancient language - *Under me doth lie another much richer than I.* Back into the garden went John with his spade to dig up even more gold coins. Swaffham's chapman - the word means pedlar or trader - used some of his money to build the north aisle of the town's big church which has its nave roof filled with angels. The likeness of John Chapman, churchwarden and rich man of business, is carved in wood on the chancel stalls, he standing with his pack on his back, accompanied by his dog, while nearby his wife minds the counter of their shop.

Success can breed jealousy which in turn may attribute the wealth of another to uncommon good fortune or, as in the case of John Chapman, to a dream. Ambrose Allen, Gent, of Bircham Newton made sure that there would be no doubt about how he achieved his success. A memorial in the little church states that this man who lived under five kings, one queen and Cromwell's Commonwealth *by his Carefull Industry Raised A Fair Fortune to his Family.*

At Wiveton on the Norfolk coast, a legend grew up to explain the good fortune of Raulf Greneway, the Tudor benefactor of the parish who left 200 marks to provide 13 pence in cash and the equivalent value in bread to a baker's dozen of poor folk every Sunday. The story arose that Raulf was a foundling child who went off to sea when he grew up, made his fortune in London and became an alderman. Raulf certainly did become an Alderman of the City of London and he was also Master of the Grocers Company whose insignia is on the brass telling of his bequest in the church, but he was a merchant's son not an abandoned babe. In the churchyard is the headstone of millwright Thomas Smith, who died in 1725, showing a millstone surrounded by the tools of his trade. A more famous folktale foundling was Sir Thomas Gresham, founder of the Royal Exchange which has a huge golden grasshopper as its emblem. One tale says that a schoolboy on his way home followed a chirping grasshopper to a hedge where he found a new-born babe. The child grew up to make his fortune in London and in memory of the escapade he adopted the grasshopper insignia and founded a famous school. In another version of the tale it was Tom's parents who found their stray infant as a result of the insect's insistent chirpings. In fact Thomas

ABOVE - *the carved figures of John Chapman, the Pedlar of Swaffham, and his wife. According to legend, the pedlar made his fortune as the result of a dream. The figures are in Swaffham church.*

was born into a wealthy family with its roots in Norfolk - his father was Lord Mayor of London as was his uncle, Sir John Gresham, the founder of a grammar school at Holt.

Many of those whose initiative led to fortune wished, like Raulf Greneway, to leave their mark on their native parish. The Cloptons of Kentwell Hall and the Martyns of Melford Place were great benefactors of Long Melford church where their brasses and memorials lie and where inscriptions ask visitors to pray for their *sowlis* and *for alle thoo sowlis yt ye seyd John is bo' nde to prey for.* In neighbouring Lavenham is the kneeling figure of Allaine Dister whose charity to the poor is described -

> *A Clothier vertuous while he was*
> *In Lavenham many a yeare*
> *For as in lyefe he loved best*
> *The poore to clothe and feede*
> *So withe the riche and all the rest*
> *He neighbourlie agreed,*
> *And did appoynt before he died*
> *A spial yearlie rent*
> *Which shoulde be every Whitsontide*
> *Amonge the poorest spent.*

John Clopton died in 1497 and Master Dister in 1534 and during that period, under the influence of Reformation ideas, the rich turned away from paying chantry priests to say prayers for their souls to helping their less fortunate fellows. Great Saxham has a memorial to merchant John Eldred who traded in Syria, Arabia and Egypt, while at Kedington, among the Barnardiston monuments is one to Thomas who pursued his entrepreneurial skills in the 17th century *and travelled to Jerusalem and the most remarkable places of Syria and Palestine.* Sir Samuel Barnardiston is also recalled in Kedington church and it was his appearance which gave rise to the term Roundhead. In 1640 he was involved in a London riot and his unfashionably short-cropped head was noticed by Queen Henrietta who exclaimed, '*What a handsome young roundhead is there!'* A man who made good but did not forget his home village or the ranks of the poor from which he came was William Newman. He enjoyed no advantage of birth - fatherless, he was raised by the parish, apprenticed to a tailor and made his fortune in the capital. For some the streets of London were indeed paved with gold. At his death in 1787 he left money *to the poor of the parish of Kettlestone for ever.*

A Norfolk man of humble origin to whom fame and fortune meant little was Johnson Jex of Letheringsett who died in 1852 aged 73 and whose death mask is in the church. His tombstone near the churchyard gate says the blacksmith-inventor-horologist was *Born in obscurity, he passed his days at Letheringsett as a village blacksmith, by the force of an original and inventive genius, combined with indomitable perseverance, he mastered some of the greatest difficulties of science; advancing from the forge to the crucible, and from the horse-shoe to the chronometer; acquiring, by mental labour and philosophic research, a vast and varied amount of mechanical skill and general knowledge. He was a man of scrupulous integrity and moral worth; but, regardless of wealth and insensible to the voice of fame. He lived and died a scientific anchorite.*

Sometimes there were gifts of land, the rent from which went to poor relief, and not only by doles of bread on Sundays. These local charity benefactions are often recorded on bequest boards hung in church towers. At Bale, where the church stands beside a grove of oaks planted to replace the great oak tree which was 12 yards round and could accommodate 20 men in its huge, hollow trunk, money was used *to Buy Blankett to Clad the Poore of Bale.* The Rector of Fyfield made the motives for his bequest plain - *That Atheism, Ignorance, Profaneness and Sin may be rooted out of the Parish, as much as may be, that the Poorer sort may have some Refreshment and all the Inhabitants cause of Thanksgiving to our good God, for some Benefit, which they and theirs may reap thereby.* As well as bread on Sundays and Christmas for a dozen poor men and women *who shall be actualy at Church to oblige them to attend Gods Worship* money was to pay a schoolmaster to teach poor

children to *read, write, cast Accompts and say the Catechism.*
Charles Dickens wrote -

> *O let us love our occupations,*
> *Bless the squire and his relations,*
> *Live upon our daily rations,*
> *And always know our proper stations.*

and in the 18th and 19th centuries people knew their station in
life, particularly in church where the squire could doze in the
privacy of his cushioned box pew. In Kedington's history-
laden church the Barnardistons could survey all from their
carved and canopied elevation and at Melton Constable the
Astley family sat in high estate in their luxurious family pew.
It was that old cavalier, Sir Jacob Astley, who spoke for every
soldier when he prayed before the battle of Edge Hill, *O Lord,*
Thou knowest how busy I must be this day; if I forget Thee, do
not Thou forget me. A later Sir Jacob Astley had fittings from
Cambridge's Corpus Christi College chapel brought to the
little church of St. Andrew at Thurning when the college's old
chapel, given by Nicholas Bacon, a Suffolk yeoman's son
who made his fortune in Elizabethan London, was torn down.
Thurning's church is a time capsule of early Victorian
England with box pews allocated to local farm families -
Burnt House farm, Rookery farm, Roundabout farm and
others - while those for the Hall and Rectory face the pulpit.
The servants and coachman from Rectory and Hall sat in their
appointed place near the tower while the commonality were
segregated on plain benches, women and girls on one side,
men and boys near the row of pegs for their caps and hats.
   Early this century at Dullingham the vicar warned that the
practice of some old folk sending children to collect their
bread dole at the church while they went off to the little chapel
on the green would not be tolerated. Standing beside the
village pond, Dullingham church had been used as a
schoolroom and poor relief office and had a charity to buy
coarse woollen cloth at Cambridge's Stourbridge Fair *to*
clothe the poor folks of the village. The charity was abused by

the landlady of the village inn and her lover to build a new coach-house. Another of the village's old customs which withered under the criticism of the vicar was that of poor women knocking on doors on St. Thomas' Eve in the hope of being given a little money for Christmas.

Those who did find fortune could ensure that their station in life was remembered in death. Dullingham's dynasty of Jeaffresons who organised candle-lit balls for the 'quality' of the county in their mansion around which they grabbed land to build a park, made the chancel of the village church their private mausoleum. They lined the walls with laudatory tablets while their bones rest in the vault below, and a general who never heard a shot fired in anger in the long wars with Napoleon sleeps hand on sword on a table tomb. The family purchased their estate with money made on their West Indies plantations, worked by Newgate convicts secured by the distribution of 'presents' to government officers and gaolers. One enterprising criminal escaped, returned to his haunts near London Bridge and was chased along the streets by the angry planter. In 1685 Christopher Jeaffreson noted in his diary the problems of transporting *one parcel of notorious villains* including a murderous soldier. He wrote, *'Upon Easter Eve about six of the clock I went to Newgate to receive the malefactors which ought to have been 47 in number; but two men and one woman were dead and one man and a woman were sick. For several reasons and pretentions four men were deteyned so that we had delivered to us but 38 prisoners, 29 men, most of them sturdy and rugged fellows, and nine women likely to make good servants. As they went down to the water-side, notwithstanding a guard of about 30 men, they committed several thefts, snatching away hats, perriwigs &c from several persons.'*

There is no reticence or false modesty about the huge memorial to Lady Anne Deane, once *of the Honorable tribe of Druries of Riddlesworth*, in Great Maplestead church. There a ghostly, white, life-size figure of the lady who died in 1633 stands over the prostrate effigy of her eldest son.

Fame and Fortune, Rags to Riches

The catalogue of her virtues relates -

> *Her shape was rare : Her beauty Exquisit*
> *Her wytt accurate : Her judgment singular*
> *Her entertayment harty : Her conversation lovely*
> *Her harte merciful : Her hand helpfull*
> *Her courses modest : Her discourses wise*
> *Her charity heavenly : Her amity constant*
> *Her practise holy : Her religion pure*
> *Her vowes lawfull : Her meditations divine*
> *Her faith unfaynd : Her hope stable*
> *Her prayers devout : Her devotions diurnail*
> *Her dayes short : Her life everlasting*

Another formidable woman must have been Lady Elizabeth Hastings who put up a set of rules for the incumbent of Howe to follow including *That he would be much in Conversation with his people, and without partiality or preferring any one to another, he would inform himself of the Spiritual Condition, the respective wants and Occasions of their Souls, and give them their portion of Meat in due Season; And by all the Wisdom and Prudence he is Master of, turn the Stream of their Affections from the momentary and vain Enjoyments of this World to the everlasting Riches and only solid Pleasures of the Next.*

One road to fame and fortune was the sea. The great curve of the East Anglian coast has attracted invaders and traders, and some boys who spent their childhood days with the salty taste of a sea breeze on their lips grew to be admirals of the king's 'navee'. Thomas Cavendish, the second Englishman to sail around the world - he captured a treasure ship on the way - lived near Trimley overlooking the estuary of the Orwell and passed on his knowledge to Richard Hakluyt, the chronicler of voyages who rejected more lucrative offers to spend his final years in tranquillity as the rector of the little Suffolk village of Wetheringsett. In the 17th century a trio of admirals who knew the smell of gunpowder but were fated not to enjoy a quiet rural retirement were born in the north Norfolk villages of Cockthorpe and Salthouse.

Tales of the deeds of Sir Christopher Myngs of Salthouse must have inspired two boys born at Cockthorpe, John Narbrough and Cloudesley Shovell, to follow his path. The three served together until Myngs was killed by the Dutch in the closing stages of the four-day battle of North Foreland. Narbrough fought off the Suffolk coast in the battle of Sole Bay, was in action with Shovell against Mediterranean corsairs, and died of fever on a mission to recover treasure in the West Indies. Shovell married Narbrough's widow and distinguished service against the French brought promotion but the life of the rich and famous admiral of the fleet was brutally ended by a poor woman for the rings on his fingers. In 1707 his ships were wrecked in a storm off the Isles of Scilly but Sir Cloudesley was washed ashore alive in a cove on St. Mary's Island where he was found by an old woman who, in a death-bed confession years later, told how she cut off his fingers for the rich rings he wore before callously murdering him and burying his body in the sand.

It was a different story for Edward Russell, who was Shovell's commander in the battle off the Normandy coast in 1692. There Shovell earned the praise for breaking the French line and Russell went home to be dismissed for failing to completely destroy the enemy fleet. He was later reinstated but resigned amid tales of corruption and devoted more of his time to his estate at Chippenham where he moved half the village to make way for his pleasure park and artificial lake. He entertained royalty, drank plenty of his favourite punch and became Earl of Orford in his comfortable old age. Another commander who got into trouble with his superiors was Admiral Vernon -'old grog' himself - the first man to issue the drink to his seamen. In 1740 he ordered that the rum ration should be diluted with water and the drink was named after the admiral's favourite old cloak of grogram which he wore as he paced the decks. He attacked the press-gang system of recruitment and tried to get better conditions for his sailors but this humane officer who wanted to reform the worst abuses of naval life was cashiered after conducting his campaign against the Admiralty in a series of anonymous pamphlets. He retired to his home beside the Orwell, became M.P. for Ipswich, died in 1757 in his seventies and was buried in Nacton church where he was joined by another ill-fated naval hero almost a century later.

Only a mile from Vernon's old home is Broke Hall where Philip Bowes Vere Broke was born in 1776. He had command of the 38-gun frigate Shannon patrolling off Boston in 1813 when he encountered the American frigate Chesapeake. In a brief battle Broke, sword in hand, led a boarding party but suffered a terrible cutlass wound to the skull which laid bare his brain. The guns of the Tower of London were fired in salute of his victory, the people of Suffolk presented him with a huge silver platter and he was given a knighthood but his injuries forced him into premature and melancholy retirement. He died in 1841 and was buried in Nacton church.

Let America know the respect she should show
To our national flag and our cannon,
And let her take heed that the Thames and the Tweed
Give us tars just as brave as the Shannon.

There were many young men whose last moments came in the deafening chaos of a naval battle. A tablet in Blyford church records the death of Edmund Freeman *killed in action with two French Frigates and a Battery off Guadaloupe in the West Indies 19th Decr 1809 aged 21 years, 5 Weeks and 4 Days* and in Horsford churchyard stands a memorial to John Pirsins, a victim of the 1797 battle of Camperdown at 11 years old.

On Southwold's Gun Hill six old cannons point their muzzles at the North Sea. They were not on the cliffs three centuries ago when Sole Bay was filled with warships and thousands of muzzle-loading cannons filled the air with the din and smoke of battle. In 1665 an English fleet under James, Duke of York, and the Earl of Sandwich had sent the Dutch scurrying home from a battle off Lowestoft with the loss of 30 ships to England's two. James, later to be the last of the Stuart kings, had command of the fleet of 101 English and French

ABOVE - *two jacks o' the clock, armoured figures which strike bells in Blythburgh (left) and Sothwold (right) churches.*

BELOW - *a row of old cannons on Gun Hill Southwold, pointing their barrels towards Sole Bay where English, French and Dutch warships clashed in battle in 1672*

ships peacefully anchored in the line eight miles long from Easton cliffs to Minsmere in May, 1672. Suddenly 90 Dutch men o' war appeared on the horizon. Alarm! Small boats shuttled groggy tars from Southwold's taverns to the warships hastily preparing for action. The Dutch sent in fireships, the French sailed clear of danger and the brave Earl was killed when his ship blew up. James' flagship, captained by Sir John Narbrough, was wrecked in the bombardment and the Duke transferred his flag to another. By sunset the protagonists had had enough and the battle ended with losses even and both sides claiming victory.

Perhaps Southwold's Jack struck his bell that night in celebration and relief at the retreat of the battered Dutch fleet. Dressed in Wars of the Roses armour, Jack still stands in the town's church dedicated to St. Edmund with its screen of angels, apostles and prophets and grotesquely carved chancel stall arm rests (another Jack o' the clock is at nearby Blythburgh). Southwold had prospered as the sea swept away the churches, shops and houses of neighbouring Dunwich but the town suffered its own disaster in 1659. The sea was not to blame, nor the Dutch, but, as at nearby Beccles and Bungay it was that scourge of towns of timber and thatch houses - fire. Prison, town hall, warehouses and houses vanished in the flames but Southwold was rebuilt with greens as firebreaks against future disasters.

It was one of eight surviving children out of 11 of a hard-up country parson whose fame outshone all the admirals of the past. His name was Horatio and he was born in 1758, the sixth child of the Rev. Edmund Nelson of Burnham Thorpe, a tiny village in the valley of the River Burn which runs towards the creeks and marshes of the Norfolk coast. The courage of the boy was soon plain. One day he disappeared into the woods and when he was rebuked by his grandmother who had feared he might have been carried off by gypsies he replied, *'Fear, grandmamma, I never saw fear, what is it?'* At boarding school he raided the headmaster's pear tree because every other boy feared to do so. When he was 12 Horatio sought service under his uncle who had command of the 64-gun Raisonnable, a ship captured from the French. War with Spain was expected after an invasion of the Falkland Islands and, as Captain Suckling prepared his ship he wrote dismissively of his nephew's chances of surviving the rigours of naval life. *'What has poor Horatio done, who is so weak, that he, above all the rest, should be sent to rough it out at sea? But let him come, and the first time we go into action, a cannon-ball may knock off his head, and provide for him at once.'* But young Horatio did not have to face any cannon-balls, the crisis blew over and the boy was packed off aboard a merchantman to the West Indies. He returned a year later thoroughly disenchanted with the idea of serving in King George's navy and it took hours of persuasion by his uncle before the future hero agreed to continue as a midshipman.

The intrepid young man was quickly noticed. He encountered a polar bear in the Arctic, was made captain of a frigate at 24 and the wars with France brought him action and fame, the loss of an arm and the sight of one eye, and a crop of deeds which became legendary. In 1801 he was second in command of a fleet ordered to the Baltic to deal with the Danes who had sided with Napoleon. The commander, Sir Hyde Parker, a man of 62, dallied in Yarmouth with his bride of 18 whose planned ball threatened to further delay departure. A stiff letter from the Admiralty got Parker under way for Copenhagen where Nelson engaged the anchored Danish ships. A signal to end the action was flown by Parker causing the Norfolk hero to exclaim, *'I have only one eye, I have a right to be blind sometimes.'* Then putting his telescope to his blind eye he added, *'I really do not see the signal!'* He turned to the captain of his flagship and ordered his own signal for closer battle to be nailed to the mast. Nelson was killed at Trafalgar in 1805 aged 47 and was buried in St. Paul's Cathedral. His sarcophagus had been intended for Cardinal Wolsey, the 11th son of an Ipswich butcher, who had found fame and fortune by a different route.

Fame and Fortune, Rags to Riches

The church at Burnham Thorpe which Nelson knew so well has a lectern and cross made from timbers of HMS Victory would he not have preferred to lie in the quiet calm of a Norfolk churchyard, its great trees rustled by winds from Scolt Head and Holkham Bay, or at Hilborough where his grandfather, father and brother were rectors and a lion and a unicorn support the Arms of James I above the legend *Exurgat Deus Dissipentur Inimici (Let God arise and his enermies be scattered)* than amid the din and tramp of tourist feet in London? Nelson deserved tranquillity after scattering so many of his king's enemies from Copenhagen to the Nile.

Holiday sailors on the meandering Waveney as it makes a great semicircle amid marshes between Beccles and Breydon Water have no fear of broadsides of cannon-balls but what does attract attention is the curious tower of the isolated church of Burgh St. Peter. It is a brick tower with each stage diminishing in size so that it resembles a child's building-block construction. A strange tale is told of a man who built a church there long ago and the spectre that haunts the churchyard waiting to collect on a deal sealed by a thumbprint in wax. Many centuries ago, it is said, a poor man sat musing on thoughts of gold when he noticed a seemingly benign old man standing behind him. He discovered, just as the Sacristan of Clare did, that the stranger was sympathetic and helpful. The stranger's offer of a loan was accepted and the agreement concluded by the unlettered rustic pressing his thumb into a tablet of wax. The poor man's life-style improved dramatically and some of his new-found wealth was spent on building a church. As the day appointed for the repayment of the loan drew near a stranger was seen loitering in the vicinity, his bony fingers clutching a parchment scroll.

But the poor man of Burgh St. Peter who had borrowed a fortune from the Devil and used some of it to build a church, saved his soul from the torments of Hell. He died, no doubt with a smile on his lips, a few hours before the loan was due and so the cheated fiend had to watch as the body was buried in consecrated soil. On the anniversary of the man's death, the spectre of a skull and skeleton returns to frighten innocent

ABOVE - *Burgh St. Peter where a devilish spirit is said to haunt the churchyard. The church has a curious tower built like a pile of children's toy blocks.*

mortals as it skulks in the churchyard in the hope of claiming the soul of a man who outwitted the Devil. The Waveney near Burgh St. Peter is also haunted by a phantom ship which, once a year, glides silently through the night with the ghost of a thieving captain at the helm. He had been entrusted with a cargo of golden guineas by a rich Beccles merchant who never saw his gold or wherry again.

Beccles, too, has a curious church tower but it is not its shape that attracts attention but its position. The Waveney valley landmark stands detached near the south-eastern corner of St. Michael's church where Nelson's father was curate at the time of his marriage to Catherine Suckling of nearby Barsham. The tower was not built at the western end of the nave because there the churchyard falls steeply away in a cliff towards Puddingmoor and the river. Near this spot, so legend tells, three men of Beccles concocted a get-rich-quick plan with three loathsome hags. The tale, set at the time of the Black Death in the mid-14th century when work on the church began, was recorded (or invented) 200 years later by a writer of verses.

> *Come out ye fleas, come out ye lice,*
> *Come out ye rats, come out ye mice.*
> *Obey the mandate all.*
> *Oh leave your nestes and walls, ye pests,*
> *From neath the floores, come out of doores*
> *And answer to the call!*

The three opportunists took their scheme to rid the town of its plague of rats to the chief magistrate who was delighted with their offer. They haggled over the price of the service with the three men knowing full well that they had the town's leader over a barrel. Eventually it was agreed that watchmaker Peter Harris, pedlar Sam Partridge and candlemaker Jonathan Betts would be paid 45,000 marks between them - a huge sum at the time. With £10,000 apiece they could live like kings. At the time the tale was set a labourer might earn £3 a year and the seamen who fought at Sole Bay three centuries (and much inflation) later were paid about £1 a month.

The trio then went to negotiate with the hags of Puddingmoor because it was in their hovel beside the river that the three cackling weavers of spells kept the key to the plan, a great iron cauldron which devoured without trace anything placed in its hot, steaming water. The ugly crones, who had once bewitched all the puddings made by the good wives of Beccles by filling them with flies, assented to play their part and put a spell on the pipes the three men would use to summon the rats to their doom. On the last day of August the watchmaker, chandler and pedlar gathered in the old market square and began piping. The vermin emerged from their nests and soon rivers of rats were flowing along the town's old streets. Down Ballygate and Blyburgate they came in search of the music, along Hungate and Saltgate scampered torrents of mice, fleas and lice. Prancing and dancing, the three pipers led the way towards the dank, stenchy shack where the hideous harridans had the cauldron already boiling over a fire. Into it jumped the verminous flood in their hundreds and thousands to vanish for ever beneath the bubbling water.

Back in the town the Portreeve waited, three piles each of 15,000 marks upon his table. The scurrying had ceased and so too had the pipers' music. Not one plaguey pest remained in Beccles town. Time passed, the magistrate waited but there was no sign of pedlar Sam, candlemaker Jonathan or even Peter the watchmaker (whose own clock must have been 150 years fast because the first portable timepiece was not made until around 1504). None dared to enquire of their whereabouts at the hovel on the riverbank where, behind its closed door, three grimy old witches cackled in delight beside an iron cauldron which would never reveal its secrets. Every year, at sunset on the last day of August, it is said, the sound of pipes can be heard in the old streets of Beccles as three skeletons rattle their bones in a jig down to the Waveney.

Beccles has its trio of true martyrs who were burned in the fires of religious persecution. Thomas Spicer aged 19 was arrested by Sir John Tyrell of Gipping for failing to go to Mass. He was thrown into Eye gaol with John Denny and

Edmund Poole and the three were burned at Beccles in May 1556, a tablet on the town's Baptist Church records their ordeal. During Mary's reign dozens of people died at the stake in East Anglia - a shoemaker at Laxfield, a servant at Walsingham, wives and weavers at Colchester, priests at Hadleigh and Cambridge and others at Bury St. Edmunds, Yoxford, Norwich and Ipswich.

For some who rose rapidly to fame (or notoriety) and fortune, the fall could be as swift as the executioner's axe upon the block. Sir John Tyrell, who hunted down Suffolk dissenters for Mary Tudor, was descended from the Sir James Tyrell of Gipping Hall who rose rapidly in the Yorkist service during the Wars of the Roses and who carries the blame for the murder of the young Edward V and Richard of York, the 'princes in the Tower'. On the orders of Richard III, the constable of the Tower of London handed over the keys to Tyrell and two accomplices for just one night and Suffolk folklore tells that it was in expiation of his crime that Sir James, one of whose antecedents is believed to be the murderer of King William Rufus, built the beautiful and remote little church at Gipping. Tyrell was executed when he plotted with Edmund de la Pole, Duke of Suffolk, whose family rose from Hull merchants almost to the throne of the realm. William de la Pole, the first Duke of Suffolk, arranged the marriage of Henry VI to a French princess, fell foul of political in-fighting but had his life spared by the king. He sailed into exile from Ipswich but his enemies stationed a squadron of ships to intercept him in the Channel and six strokes severed his head as he stretched his neck over the gunwale. The de la Poles vanished violently from history, one brother headed a revolt and was killed in battle, Edmund, the last Duke of Suffolk of their line, was executed by Henry VIII, another died fighting for the French and a fourth confined in the Tower of London. Their father had died in his bed and his tomb and effigy lie in Wingfield church beneath an old helmet surmounted by a grinning Saracen's head. Close by is the wooden effigy of his grandfather, Michael, the builder of Wingfield's moated castle, who died of dysentery at Harfleur.

The Suffolk dukedom also brought tragedy to those who took the title after the de la Poles. Charles Brandon aroused the anger of Henry VIII by taking the king's sister, Mary, who had been married briefly to the King of France. When Mary died in 1533 she was buried in the Abbey of St. Edmund until her brother forced its closure and her tomb was moved to another church. Brandon then married his ward who gave him two sons. They went off to study at Cambridge, caught the plague and died the same day. The dukedom of Suffolk ended with Henry Grey who married a daughter of Brandon and Mary. Grey conspired to put his daughter, Lady Jane, on the throne but the plot collapsed and a few days after tragic Jane, the queen for nine days, was executed, he, too, lost his head.

ABOVE - *the effigy of John de la Pole, a Duke of Suffolk who did not lose his head, in Wingfield church. He rests against a Saracen's head and above is a helmet decorated with a grinning Saracen. Beside him is his wife, Elizabeth Plantagenet.*

Another man - no noble but the son of a staymaker - who, but for a stroke of good fortune, would have lost his head was Tom Paine of Thetford, a supporter of the American colonies in their fight for independence and author of 'Rights of Man'. His lucky escape from the guillotine happened in 1794 when he was locked up in Paris during the French Revolution. During the day a mark would be chalked on the cell doors of those condemned to die and they would be taken away during the night. The door of Tom's room was marked when it was wide open and pushed outward against the wall. When the door was closed the mark of death was unseen on the inside so 'the destroying angel passed by'. Not that Tom believed in angels. He wrote, '*I do not believe in the creed professed by any church that I know of. My own mind is my own church. All national institutions of churches appear to me no other than human inventions set up to terrify and enslave mankind and to monopolise power and profit.*' He died on the other side of the Atlantic and the statue of him in his home town was given by the Thomas Paine Society of America.

Radical Tom would have shed no tears for Elizabeth, Countess Rivers of Melford Hall. Within a year of gaining the title, the royalist old lady's world began to fall apart - Civil War, her estates ransacked and she fined by Parliament, she died aged 70 in a debtors' gaol and her Melford home was later acquired by the family of sea-faring Hyde Parkers. Above some rough wood benches in Cowlinge church it is recorded *That at a visitacion houlden at Cowlinge the 2 day of July in the yeer of O Lord 1618 it was inacted with the consente of the then churchwardens that it shulde be lawful for Thomas Wolrych Esquier to erect and build up certain seates behind the north churche dore for the use of the keeper of the correction house in Cowlinge aforesaide and the prisoners theirin and so to continewe.* The houses of correction and bridewells for the 'indolent poor' to be 'brought up in labour' were part of the countess's world which radicals like Tom Paine helped to change. Tom, who once led a campaign for more pay for excisemen, would have approved the words which, although cut into the wall of Eye church porch in 1601, remain a wise guide for modern man -

Seale not to soone lest thou repente to late,
Yet helpe thy frend, but hinder not thy state.
If ought thou lende or borrow, truly pay,
Ne give, ne take advantage, though thou may,
Let conscience by thy guide, so helpe thy frend,
With loving peace and concord make thy end.

Tales of Love and Marriage, Some Rough, Some Smooth

Long ago there was a strange belief that had unhappy wives hurrying to the Norfolk village of Winfarthing and the husbands of the neighbourhood to carefully check their chandler's bills. It was all because of the curious properties attributed to the Good Sword of Winfarthing which was said to have belonged to a felon who had claimed sanctuary in the village church. When the robber departed he left his sword behind and it became the object of 'vow makings, crouchinges and kissinges' by people from far and near. Some came because the sword was believed to assist in finding lost goods, particularly stolen or strayed horses. But it was when a wife set a candle before Winfarthing's sword Sunday after Sunday that a husband had reason to be alarmed. It might indicate that she had lost something. But it could be the signal that she wanted to be rid of her spouse because the sword was believed to have the power to shorten a man's life. To gain the help of the sword's powers to end a marriage, a wife had to burn a candle before it each and every Sunday for a year. One wonders how many marital arguments were caused by the wives of Winfarthing trotting off to church or husbands meticulously checking on the use of candles.

An alternative way of being rid of a husband was to make a gift of a peck of oats to St. Wilgefortis, better known to wives as St. Uncumber. It was believed she could unencumber a good wife of a bad husband by packing him off to the devil on a horse. The mythical saint was said to have been a pagan king of Portugal's daughter who prayed to be made ugly when her father wanted to marry her off. As a result she grew a beard which had the effect of frightening away the suitor and causing her angry father to have her put to death. Winfarthing's sword has disappeared but St. Uncumber with bearded face can be seen in Worstead church with another saint of doubtful background, St. William of Norwich, an alleged victim of ritual murder like St. Robert of Bury St.

Edmunds and little St. Hugh of Lincoln.

Another way of breaking the bond of an unhappy marriage in days before divorce was widespread was for a husband to take his wife to market 'as if she were a brood mare or milch cow' and there sell her to the highest bidder. The wife sale was usually arranged with husband and wife having agreed to part and the bidder having been informed of the forthcoming 'sale'. The market auction was a public proclamation of the parting - a statement by the husband that he was not responsible for any future debts she might accumulate and that both were free to marry again. A farmer of Stowupland sold his wife to a neighbour in 1787 for five guineas. He was so pleased with the bargain he gave his ex-wife a guinea to buy a new dress and had the bells of Stowmarket rung in celebration. A few years before in Norfolk a man had received his new wife at a crossroads, she without a stitch of clothing on her. This was to show that he took her free of any debts that her previous spouse may have run up. Then off to church went the happy couple, she with a dress to cover her modesty, to be lawfully joined in wedlock.

For the wife who misplaced her best pewter platter there was an alternative to visiting Winfarthing. She could invoke the help of St. Anthony of Padua in the same way that she might ask the blessing of St. Margaret of Antioch in time of childbirth, St. Apollonia when she had toothache, or St. Erasmus when her children had stomach ache. Starry-eyed young lovers could seek the aid of St. Valentine and should their union prove to be childless, the wife could go to Bury St. Edmunds, borrow a white bull, decorate it with ribbons and flowers, and lead it around the abbey. Then she would go to the shrine of St. Edmund and pray that the oblation would result in her marriage being blessed with children.

When the body of Amy Dudley was found lying with a broken neck at the bottom of a flight of stairs in Cumnor Hall near Oxford gossip rapidly created a legend. The Norfolk beauty had been murdered, they said, so that the husband who had grown tired of her might become king. Amy, daughter of Sir John Robsart, might have lived out her life quietly had not

Robert Kett, an affluent yeoman farmer involved in the tannery business, put himself at the head of a rebellion that began at Wymondham in 1549. An army marched to put Kett and his men in their place and leading the king's array was John Dudley, Earl of Warwick, who brought his son, Robert, along to get experience of a battle. The royal army camped near Amy's home, Stanfield Hall, and she soon caught the eye of Robert who was then only 16 years old. A year later they were married in the presence of King Edward VI. But in the Dudley blood was a lust for power. Warwick became Duke of Northumberland, plotted the fall and execution of the king's uncle and drew the reins of power into his own hands as the young king's health failed. As death closed in on Edward in the summer of 1553 another of the Dudley sons was married to tragic Jane Grey, daughter of the Duke of Suffolk, her parents beating her into acceptance of the match. The plan collapsed as Mary rallied support at Framlingham castle, and the two fathers and newly-weds lost their heads.

Amy's husband, too, had a taste of life in the Tower until he was released to take up a quiet life in Norfolk. Then everything changed when Elizabeth came to the throne in 1558. Robert hastened away to the pleasures of the young queen's court where he soon enjoyed royal favour. Tongues began to wag and there were rumours that unhappy Amy was being dosed with poison to open Robert's path to a royal wedding. Two years later Amy was dead. Was it murder, suicide or accident? Amy's fall down the stairs may have been caused by her long illness and an inquest said her death was an accident, but the whispers of foul play persisted and 250 years later Sir Walter Scott used the tale in his novel 'Kenilworth'. The scandal ended Dudley's hopes of becoming Elizabeth's consort and instead of a crown he received the Earldom of Leicester. It is said that the ghost of sad, neglected Amy appeared before Dudley shortly before his own death and that her spirit haunts the scene of her unhappiness at Cumnor as well as Rainthorpe Hall near Tasburgh, a place of happiness for her when her family lived there.

The Stanfield Hall which Amy knew has gone and the

present hall has its associations with the bloody events of a double murder which happened on a November night in 1848. The house was the home of Isaac Jermy, the Recorder of Norwich. One of his tenant-farmers was James Rush, a man with a violent temper who wanted the hall for himself. Wearing a disguise, Rush hid in the bushes armed with a shotgun and waited for the Recorder to emerge for his evening stroll. When Jermy appeared, Rush gunned him down, then rushed into the house where he killed the lawyer's son and wounded Mrs. Jermy and a maid. He then ran home, leaving a note to throw suspicion onto others. Rush's angry dispute with Mr. Jermy was common knowledge and when his mistress, the governess of his children, told of his long absence with a gun on the night of the murder, Rush's fate was sealed. He was publicly executed at Norwich Castle in front of a vast crowd of thousands of onlookers.

Twenty years before the Stanfield Hall murders, thousands of people had turned out to watch the hanging of another murderer at Bury St. Edmunds following the strange revelations at the trial of William Corder. What caught the public imagination about the otherwise unremarkable murder trial was the way the crime came to light, causing the name of Corder and his victim, Maria Marten, to enter folklore's long memory. The events centred on the Red Barn at Polstead where Maria met her lover in the belief that they would go away together and be married. Maria, the daughter of a mole-catcher, was 25. But she was no innocent country maiden. As the result of her affair with the farmer's son she had had a child which died in infancy but after the meeting in the barn in May, 1827 she was never seen alive again. The months passed and inquiries about Maria's whereabouts were answered by Corder saying she had left the area and that he intended to join her and make Maria his wife. He went off to London where he was arrested after his crime was revealed by Maria's stepmother in a way Corder could not have foreseen. Mrs. Marten had been unconvinced by Corder's tales and she suspected that there had been foul play at the lovers' last meeting. She had a dream which indicated the exact spot where the murdered Maria was buried in the Red Barn and at her insistence a search was made and the body uncovered. Corder admitted his guilt shortly before his execution and macabre relics of the affair are in Moyses Hall museum, a 12th century building in Bury St. Edmunds that during its long history has been a medieval bank, a house of correction and a police station. Maria's tale became a popular melodrama which was performed in barns and halls all over the country by travelling players, she being portrayed as the young and blameless maiden brutally murdered by the local, lustful ne'er-do-well.

Another Suffolk 'heroine' who caught the popular imagination in a romantic but tragic tale was Margaret Catchpole whose smuggler-lover died in her arms in the chill of dawn on a lonely beach. The Rev. Richard Cobbold of Wortham wrote his story in 1845, weaving actual events into his tale of romance, treachery and death, and in Christchurch Mansion museum at Ipswich documents telling of the deeds of the real Margaret are to be seen. The tale is that Margaret fell in love with Will Laud, a smuggler, whom she begged to give up his criminal activities and settle down to married life. They planned to make a new life together beyond the reach of the excise men, and to join her lover she stole a horse and rode the 70 miles to London in less than nine hours. Unfortunately she was tracked down, sent back to face trial for the theft and was sentenced to death but this was commuted to transportation for seven years in Australia.

While in Ipswich gaol she plotted her escape and was united once more with Laud. The two lovers, disguised as sailors, hurried to the coast near Sudbourne where a ship would carry them away to freedom in Holland. But tragedy overtook them, the excise men and the Ipswich gaoler caught up with them on the beach at dawn just as the boat was approaching the shore. Laud refused to allow his love to be taken back to jail, a pistol shot rang out and he fell dead at her feet, shot through the heart. Once more Margaret was condemned to death and again the sentence was mercifully reduced to transportation, but this time for the term of her life.

In Australia she found happiness at last, so the tale goes, as the wife of a rich man. The real Margaret Catchpole who rode a stolen horse to London was sentenced to transportation and scaled the wall of Ipswich prison on the night of March 25, 1800. She was described at the time of her escape as a woman of *'about 38 years of Age - Swarthy Complexion - very dark Eyes and Hair - hard featured'*. A year later she arrived in Australia where her death was recorded in May, 1819 at the age of 58 and unmarried. The Margaret Catchpole portrayed in the reverend gentleman's imaginative writing is the romantic image that will endure in Suffolk folklore and legend.

A pistol shot outside a theatre in April, 1779 ended the passionate infatuation of James Hackman whose tenure as rector of Wiveton must be among the briefest anywhere. The former soldier received the living of the Norfolk village when he was 27 but he soon left for a tragic confrontation in London with the object of his desires. She was Martha Ray, the long time mistress and mother of children by Lord Sandwich, who is best remembered for giving his name to a snack of a slice of beef between toast. Miss Ray, a London staymaker's daughter, did not respond to Hackman's advances. One night, as she came out of a theatre after seeing the play 'Love in a Village', Hackman shot her in the head and then turned another pistol on himself but inflicted only a minor wound. Hackman gave up all earthly tenure when he was hanged at Tyburn 50 days after his institution at Wiveton.

For the wife who dissolved her marriage by violence the result could be cruel death. In 1608 the rector of Rockland St. Peter was murdered by his curate with the connivance of the rector's wife. She was burned and her lover, who had killed their child, was hanged and drawn - murder of a husband was then considered a crime akin to treason. A happier tale is that of a vicar of West Rudham who was forced to 'put away' his wife when Queen Mary re-imposed clerical celibacy. His wife married another man but when Elizabeth came to the throne and priests were allowed to marry again, the vicar took her back. The reactions of her temporary husband are not recorded.

Folklore has preserved many bizarre methods by which an East Anglian maid might discover her destined mate. She could throw apple peel over her shoulder and it would spell the first letter of his name, or she could put a two-leaf clover in her shoe and the next man she met or one with the same name was the one meant for her. Another way was to put a pod of peas over the kitchen door and the first man to enter was sure to be her destined companion. To check on the constancy of a sweetheart's vows of love it was recommended that the girl should throw a pip on the fire. If it made a bang he was true, if it burned silently his words were false.

ABOVE - *Matoaka Rebecka Pocahontas, the Red Indian princess who married the English adventurer John Rolfe and lived briefly at his Heacham home, depicted in the village church. She had intervened to prevent the execution of Capt. John Smith and had aided the Jamestown colony. Rolfe's first wife and child had died after a shipwreck.*

Various curious rituals were said to work only on St. Mark's Eve (April 24). One was for a girl to make a cake with an eggshell full of salt, an eggshell of wheatmeal and another of barleymeal. This had to be done alone and without a word being spoken and then the cake was cut into three sections and a piece of each part eaten. The rest was placed under her pillow and at midnight the girl had to go to bed backwards where she would see an image of her love. If she saw nothing she was destined to remain a spinster. Also at midnight she could go into the garden and sow hemp seed as she chanted the words, *'Hemp seed I sow, hemp seed, grow; He that is my true love come after me and mow.'* This would cause her future spouse to appear with a scythe. Another spell which only worked in silence was to place two pewter pots upside down on the hearth then go up to bed backwards. In the morning whatever was under the pots would indicate the trade of the maiden's destined husband - soil for a farm labourer, a scrap of wood for a carpenter. And should a younger sister marry first it was expected that the elder, defeated in the race to the altar, would dance a jig in the swine trough.

East Anglia has a multitude of links with the founding of America. Many men and women crossed the Atlantic to begin a new life or to escape religious persecution. One of Abraham Lincoln's forebears was a weaver at Hingham; John Winthrop, the founder of Boston, came from a rich clothier family at Groton, and in Manuden church a memorial to Sir William Waad, who watched over Guy Fawkes in the Tower of London, claims his father was the 'English Columbus'.

A romantic link with the early days of the American colonies is recalled by the memorial in Heacham church to Pocahontas, the Red Indian princess who intervened to save the lives of Capt. John Smith and other Virginian settlers. In 1614 she married John Rolfe, a Norfolk man from Heacham, in the fledgling colony at Jamestown. The couple returned to England where Pocahontas became a celebrity in London society but her health rapidly deteriorated in the English climate. She died in 1617 aged only 22 just before she was due to sail back to America. Rolfe prospered in the tobacco

Tales of Love and Marriage

ABOVE - left, parental authority being administered to a child's bare rump. One of the many fine 14th century woodcarvings in Norton church. Right, the shrouded skeleton that stands holding an hour glass in one hand and a scythe in the other as a grim reminder of mortality in St. Andrew's Church, Little Barningham. The original, which had been in place for hundreds of years, was stolen in 1996. Carved on the panels of one side of the special pew are the words -

FOR COVPLES JOYND IN WEDLOCKE, AND MY FREINDS,
THAT STRANGER IS THIS SEATE DID I INTEND, BVILT
AT THE COSTE AND CHARGE OF STEVEN CROSBEE

On another panel beneath the disconcerting skeleton are the cautionary words -

ALL YOU THAT DOE THIS PACE PASS BY
AS YOV ARE NOWE EVEN SOE WAS I
REMEMBER DEATH FOR YOU MUST DYE
AND AS I AM SOE SHALL YOU BE
PREPARE THEREFORE TO FOLLOW ME
16 ANNO DOMINI 40

trade but was killed by Indians a few years later. The modern memorial to Pocahontas shows her in early Stuart costume.

A warning against parting young lovers is given in an old tale of a Suffolk farmer's daughter sent away by her father to put a stop to her romance. The young man pined for his love and died of a broken heart. A few weeks later he appeared to his lost love, carried her back to her father's house on horseback and as she clung to him during the night ride she tied her handkerchief around his cold head. When her incredulous father heard the tale he had the sexton open the young man's grave and to his dismay found the handkerchief around the head of the mouldering body. When the girl was told what had happened and that it had been her lover's ghost that had carried her off on horseback she too soon died of grief.

A pair of young lovers who were forced to meet in secret are remembered by the tale of a ghost of a drummer boy which haunts Hickling Broad. He would skate across the ice to be with his sweetheart but one winter night the ice gave way and he was drowned but, they say, his drumming can still be heard on cold February nights as the phantom skater searches for this true love. Another old tale of parted lovers is set only a giant's stone throw from Tom Hickathrift's alleged Marshland grave at Tilney All Saints. Now a ruined church and a scattering of houses mark Islington, once the home of a bailiff's beautiful daughter, whose love long ago for the squire's son was celebrated in ballad. He was sent away to London as an apprentice while in Islington the bailiff's daughter regretted having coyly rejected his advances. Seven years later she set off for London to search for him and on the road met a rider who asked about the bailiff's daughter. She told him that the object of his inquiry was dead whereupon the man threatened to go to some far country. All ended happily when the maid of Islington revealed her identity with pledges of undying love.

For lovers of a merry jest was the tale of Suffolk Nell, a beautiful but cunning maiden, and how she captured the wealthy lawyer who had taken advantage of her services as his housekeeper. When she discovered that her apron seemed to be getting noticeably shorter, she informed her employer of her plight. The lawyer swore that the Devil could carry him off to Hell if he failed to make her his bride. But when seven of the nine months passed without a wedding and he began to court a lady of quality, Nell made her plans. She waited in the wood through which the lawyer would return home and there, with horns on her head and disguised as the Devil, she ambushed him late one night. The lawyer was given a day to honour his promise or, so the 'devil' warned him, he would be consigned to Hell. Next day they were wed and lived happily ever after.

At Walsham-le-Willows it was the custom to put a garland on the memorial in the church to Mary Boyce who died unmarried in 1685 when she was 20. On the church wall is a wooden crant bearing her name, a carved skull, bone, and heart and arrow - it is said she died of a broken heart. At Navestock, where the church oak tower survived a German land-mine explosion in 1940, Jane Radcliffe, who died at 15, is described on her memorial as *So faire a blossome so exquisitely good, That I want words to make it understood.* When John Glover became parson of Shottisham in 1618 he wrote some depressing lines of Latin in the register saying that each generation in turn produces offspring more wicked and evil than their parents and that his was an age of thoroughly corrupt morals. When his wife Rose died he placed a brass plate in the church floor with a verse to her memory between a rose and a sunflower -

As wither'd Rose its fragrant sent retains
So beinge dead her vertue still remains
Shee is not dead but chang'd, ye good ner dies
But rather shee is sun like set to rise.

A narrow country lane from Shottisham leads to the lonely church at Ramsholt from whose round tower the sexton used to watch on Sundays for the approach of the vicar in his boat. The church has a brick floor and box pews and outside a row of 18th century gravestones carved with skulls and bones. This was smuggler country in Margaret Catchpole's day and in many places the myth grew up that such symbols of mortality on headstones indicated the grave of a contraband runner. The spade, skull and coffin on old Jephtha Weller's stone probably indicates that he was the local gravedigger. Smugglers were not the sort to advertise, even in death.

Not every husband would have agreed with a bishop who told Queen Elizabeth in a sermon that while some women were wiser than many men, there were others who were *foolish, wanton, tattlers, triflers, witless, feeble, rash, proud, tale-bearers, eavesdroppers, rumour-raisers, evil tongued and in every way doltified with the dregs of the devil's dunghill.*

In the Broadland church of Martham is a memorial to Christopher and Alice Burraway which says enigmatically that Alice *by hir life was my sister, my mistress, my mother and my wife.* She died in 1729 aged 76 and he the following year at 59. This puzzling statement gave rise to an odd tale whereby Alice bore a child (so mother) by an incestuous relationship with her father (so sister). To avoid scandal the child was passed off as a foundling but returned as a man to become the steward of his sister-mother's farm (so mistress) and later they were married (so wife). But Alice recognised a mark on his body, realised the dreadful truth and died. Christopher probably intended the words to be interpreted without such salacious gossip. It seems likely that his parents died when he was young and Alice was his stepfather's wife and of an age to be looked upon as an elder sister. As his stepmother she would have been his mistress in the sense of having authority over him during his late childhood and although she was 18 years his senior, marriage to an older women was not uncommon.

A very old test of a happy marriage was the award of the Dunmow flitch of bacon to a couple who, for a year and a day, had lived in perfect harmony without regret or quarrel. The custom is mentioned in Chaucer's 'Canterbury Tales' and Langland's 'The Vision of Piers the Plowman', both written in the 14th century. In the latter the dreamer is told that marriage should be for love not money, girls should not wed doddering old men and virile young males must not marry wealthy old widows. The Dunmow prize is attributed to Robert Fitzwalter, the baron who attacked Binham Priory and led the opposition to tyrannical King John at St. Edmund's shrine. Exile, crusader, and Marshal of the Host of the Lord and Holy Church which forced John to put his seal to Magna Carta, Robert lies buried near the altar of Little Dunmow church which is all that remains of the Augustinian priory. In the church is an effigy of one of Robert's daughters who, legend says, was Maid Marion Fitzwalter of Robin Hood and Sherwood Forest fame or, alternatively, poisoned by King John when she resisted his amorous advances. In the chancel is the old flitch chair on which the bacon-winning couple were ceremonially paraded. Thomas and Ann Shakeshaft of Wethersfield were carried in the chair in June 1751 *having first kneelt down upon two bare stones within the Church door, & taken the said Oath pursuant to the Antient Custom, in manner & form prescribed -*

You shall swear by the Custom of our Confession
That you never made any Nuptial Transgression
Since you were married Man & Wife,
By Houshold Brawls or Contentious Strife;
Or otherwise in Bed, or at Board,
Offended each other in deed or in word;
Or since the Parish Clerk said Amen,
Or in a Twelve month and a day,
Repented not in thought any way,
But Continued true and in Desire,
As when you joyned Hands in holy Quire;
If to these Conditions without all fear,
Of your own accord you will freely swear,
A Gammon of Bacon you shall receive,
And bear it hence with Love & good Leave;
For this is our Custom at Dunmow well known,
Though the sport be ours the Bacon's your own.

After the closure of the priory the tradition continued intermittently until it was revived by the Victorian Harrison Ainsworth who wrote a novel about the custom. On the floor of Little Dunmow church a brass records the fate of John Wylde, the son of a judge sent to the country in the hope of escaping the plague in the capital. It was in vain - John *brought hither for a private apartmt dureing the rageing pestilence at London departed this life 8 Oct, 1665 aged about 9 moneths.*

Only a few miles from Dunmow is Finchingfield where tourists go to gaze upon old cottages, duckpond and stream, and take their refreshment in the Green Man Inn. High on the hill is the church where a memorial tells of the vow of silence taken by a Puritan husband - he refused to speak to anyone for seven years. William Kempe *Pious, Just, Hospitable, Master of him selfe soe much that what others scarce doe by force and penalties, Hee did by a Voluntary constancy Hold his peace Seaven yeares.* Old William, squire of Spains Hall, accused his young wife, *a woman of a Chast life & Religion, Discreet in both,* of infidelity and to atone for his unjust charge he swore not to utter another word for seven years. The tale is that ill-luck dogged him from then on. He dug a pond to mark the end of the first year and some of his servants drowned in it, and when he fell off his horse he lay helpless in the rain all night rather than shout for help. On another occasion his refusal to speak resulted in a comedy of errors. By chance he had overheard some robbers plotting to attack his home so he sent a servant ahead with a written message of warning. Unfortunately the servant could not read and when he arrived at the hall the rain had ruined the writing. The hall servants assumed their master needed aid so left the house unguarded for the robbers to loot at their leisure.

Kempe, who died in 1628 aged 73, five years after his wife's death, appointed the Puritan Stephen Marshall as vicar. Marshall had been educated at Emmanuel College in Cambridge, a centre of radical religious ideas such that the road outside was known as Preachers Street. Marshall became embroiled in politics and when the Civil War began his exhortations to Parliament's regiments before the Battle of Edge Hill ensured that Sir Jacob Astley and the royalist side would have a busy day indeed. Like Cromwell, Marshall's body was dug up from Westminster Abbey when the monarchy was restored and thrown into the common pit. Thomas Marriott died at Finchingfield a century later. For him youthful *life glided smooth adown its easy way* and it was his opinion *That Wealth, Wit, Wisdom are a vain pretence.*

Marriage held little happiness for the Rev. Alexander Gough of Thorpe-le-Soken, close to the creeks of the Essex coast. He fell for the beautiful Catherine Canham who lived nearby in a hall above the marshes that surround Hamford Water. They were married in 1745 but Kitty soon abandoned the quiet life as wife to a country parson and vanished with a rich and handsome young man of noble birth. They were married bigamously and for a few years travelled the Continent and lived in style in Italy. Then Kitty fell ill and on her deathbed she revealed the truth and made her lover promise that she would be buried at Thorpe-le-Soken. Her embalmed corpse was put in a packing case for the long journey to Essex and in the guise of a merchant named Williams, her 'husband' almost succeeded in his plan. But some inquisitive customs officers opened the chest to find the body of the parson's erring wife and the mystery of Kitty's disappearance was solved as was the identity of her aristocratic lover. He was Lord Dalmeny, son of Lord Rosebery, and upon him fell the wrath of the wronged Mr. Gough. The beautiful woman who had brought happiness and sorrow to both men was buried at Thorpe when she was a little over 30 years old and Lord Dalmeny followed Kitty to the grave five years later aged 30 and legally unmarried.

Wetheringsett, where Richard Hakluyt passed the final years of his life in rural calm, was rocked by a scandal at the end of the 19th century which caused the hasty passing of an Act of Parliament. For several years couples had been married in the church at one of Suffolk's prettiest villages, or so they thought, but it came to light that in the eyes of the law these men and women were not joined in wedlock. The problem was that the rector, George Ellis, a former tailor and bishop's butler, was an impostor. For pretending to be a priest and conducting false marriages he was sent to prison and Parliament quickly passed a law making the bogus weddings valid. A footbridge across the brook leads into the churchyard where a skeleton sits upon an open coffin. This macabre sight near the porch is carved on the headstone of three sisters of the Peck family who all died young late in the 18th century. By a strange twist of fate only a few feet away is a stone recalling three more Peck sisters of a later generation who died young and unmarried in successive years.

Landlady Martha Blewit of the Swan Inn, Baythorn End, obviously enjoyed being married - she was a bride nine times. A tablet in Birdbrook church records that Martha, who died in 1681 *was Wife of nine Husbands succesively, but the ninth outlived her. The Text to her Funeral Sermon was Last of all the Woman died also.* The same memorial tells that another parishioner, Robert Hogan, was *the Husband of Seven Wives successively.* Elizabeth Hyam of Boxford was more moderate in the number of her marriages, she married four times and was widowed four times. Her memorial tells that she *by a Fall, that brought on a Mortification, was at last hastened to her End on the 4th May 1748 in her 113th year.* Thomas Dorling of Bury St. Edmunds had only one wife, Mary, and a memorial on the wall of St. Mary's church states succinctly - *Say what a Wife should be and She was that.*

In the thatched church of St. Andrew at Bramfield a memorial set into the floor tells the sad tale of Bridgett Applewhaite who decided to risk getting married for the second time after enjoying the freedom of widowhood only to collapse as if thunder-strook into the arms of her intended new husband. Her memorial states - *After the Fatigues of a Married Life, Born by her with Incredible Patience, For four Years and three Quarters, bating three*

Weeks, And after the Enjoyment of the Glorious Freedom Of an Easy and Unblemisht Widowhood, For four Years and Upwards, She Resolved to run the Risk of a Second Marriage-Bed. Fate, however, intervened and Bridgett did not have to endure the fatigues of a second marriage. *But DEATH forbad the Banns - And having with an Apoplectick Dart (The same Instrument, with which he had Formerly Dispatcht her mother,) Touch't the most Vital part of her Brain; She must have fallen Directly to the Ground, (as one Thunder strook,) If she had not been Catch't and Supported by her Intended Husband. Of which Invisible Bruise, After a Struggle for above Sixty Hours, With that Grand Enemy of Life, (But the certain and Mercifull Friend to Helpless Old Age,) In terrible Convulsions, Plaintive Groans, or Stupefying Sleep without Recovery of her Speech, or Senses, She dyed, on the 12th day of Sept.in ye Year of Our Lord 1737 and of her own Age 44.* A few feet away, under the armoured figure of her husband, old breastplates and helmets, is the effigy of Elizabeth Coke lying upon tasselled cushions and cradling a babe in her arms. She, one feels, would not have approved of such anti-marital sentiments.

ABOVE - *the massive stone keep of the William d'Aubigny's fortess at Castle Rising which is said to be haunted by the wails of remorse of Queen Isabella who plotted with her lover, Roger Morimer, to murder her husband, King Edward II in the dungeons of Berkeley Castle. Her son, Edward III, confined her to Castle Rising.*

Ghosts, Phantoms, Spooks and Spectres

Ghosts and phantoms abound in East Anglia, or at least tales of them do. Spectral smugglers haunt deserted moonlit beaches, coaches drawn by headless horses gallop along lonely roads, the ruined castles and monasteries all have their ancient spooks and in many old pubs and coaching inns not all the spirits are in bottles.

The great square stone keep of Castle Rising is haunted by the pitiless Isabella, the queen who had her weak husband, Edward II, hideously murdered in the dungeons of Berkeley castle. In 1326 she and her lover Roger Mortimer had landed with an army at Ipswich and deposed the king. But when her son, Edward III, asserted his authority, Mortimer was executed and the French she-wolf was sent to a comfortable retirement at Castle Rising. It is said that sometimes the wind from the Wash picks up Isabella's wails of anguish and remorse to echo them around the deserted castle. The fortress was built by William d'Aubigny who married a widowed queen of England and, as Earl of Arundel, greatly advanced the family fortunes. He was known as William of the Strong Hand in commemoration of a legendary feat of bravery. The beautiful widowed queen of France fell for brave William but he refused her because he was pledged to marry Adela, the widow of Henry I. Annoyed, the French queen confronted the unarmed William with a ferocious lion. The English knight calmly wrapped his cloak around his arm, thrust it into the roaring beast's mouth and pulled out its tongue which he sent to his hostess as a gift. In Castle Rising village the Trinity Hospital, founded in 1616 by the Earl of Northampton, is for 12 ladies of gentler repute. They had to be honest widows of 56 years or more, *no common beggar, harlot, scold, drunkard, or haunter of taverns and alehouses.* The Jacobean gateway, chapel and homes are grouped around a central courtyard and the benefactor's badge is embroidered on the scarlet cloaks worn with tall black hats by the sisters when they cross the road to church.

The notoriously cruel turncoat, Geoffrey de Mandeville, Earl of Essex, was hit by an arrow when he led his outlaw gang of cut throats in an attack on Burwell castle in 1144. Earthwork mounds are all that remain of the unfinished stronghold built by Stephen to pen the bandit baron in his Fenland lair and on wild winter nights, it is said, Mandeville's dying curses are borne on the wind. In the nearby churchyard a stone recalls the 18th century tragedy of 78 villagers killed by fire at a puppet show in a barn. Baconsthorpe Castle was built in the 15th century by the Heydon family and here the ripples which disturb the waters of the moat and lake are said to be caused by a spectral sentry playfully throwing plum stones!

The ghost of Anne Boleyn, second of the six wives of Henry VIII, haunts Blickling Hall - on the anniversary of her execution in 1536 she arrives with her head on her lap in a coach drawn by headless horses and driven by a headless coachman. The coach disappears as Anne's spirit wanders the huge house built almost a century after her death by Lord Chief Justice Sir Henry Hobart. Another phantom coach, also drawn by a team of headless horses, gallops along Norfolk lanes on the night of May 19, the date of Anne's death at the hands of a specially hired French swordsman. It carries the spectre of her father, Sir Thomas Boleyn, Earl of Wiltshire, who is doomed to make the frantic annual journey for a thousand years. He, too, has his head tucked under his arm - perhaps in sympathy with his daughter's unjust fate - as he crosses the river Bure from one bank to another by a predestined route over all the bridges downstream between Blicking and Wroxham Broad. Another queen who rides the country lanes in a coach drawn by headless horses is Mary Tudor who makes moonlight trips to her cruel accomplice, Tyrell of Gipping Hall.

On the Suffolk coast at Oulton the ghost of an unfaithful wife is said to walk clutching a cup of poison in her hands. She had been caught in the arms of her lover by the husband they thought was out of the way chasing foxes. In the inevitable argument the lover killed the husband and the guilty pair hurriedly fled, abandoning a fatherless young daughter who had knowledge of their crime. Later a black coach pulled up at the house, the daughter was bundled into it and driven away to a fateful meeting with the mother who had a cup of poison ready.

Perhaps the unfortunate squire of Oulton knew the renowned foxhunter of Cantley, Robert Gilbert, whose memorial claims that he had a reputation as a mighty hunter, greater even than the mythical Nimrod. This hunter *in wise Frugality, LUXURIANT, In justice, & good acts, EXTRAVIGANT, To all ye world, a UNIVERSALL FRIEND,* was, so his epitaph declares, a foe to none except the Norfolk wildlife. He died in 1714 when he was 59 -

> *Tho' hundreds to ye ground, he oft has Chac'd,*
> *That Subtile FOX, DEATH, Earth'd him here at last.*
> *And left a Fragrant Scent, so sweet behind,*
> *That ought to be persu'd by all Mankin*d.

Yet another phantom coach driven by a naughty squire was said to cause frights in the lanes near Reydon while another pulled by headless horses appears once a year near Beccles and some say it is old Hugh Bigod racing home to Bungay castle. At the nearby church at Shadingfield they say you can see the bells being swung by an invisible phantom, and so you can but it is an illusion caused by the louvred windows of the tower where the red brick patches are locally attributed to repairs made necessary by a wayward Roundhead cannonball. At Worstead a spectral bell-ringer scared a man to death one winter night. The tale is that some merry-makers got to talking of the phantom which local legend said tolled a bell at midnight. One of the party, overflowing with beery bravado, volunteered to confront the spook and departed alone to the church tower. When his companions, anxious at his long absence, found the ghost-hunter he was gibbering in terror in the belfry and close to death.

George Mace was a hunter who pursued his quarry by moonlight. He met his end one night when he set out with some accomplices intent on poaching some birds from an estate near Watton. They had planned to meet at deserted Breckles Hall before dawn to share their haul but George did not keep the appointment. While the other poachers waited for their leader they heard a coach dash up to the door of the old house, lights were flashed, the coach door was opened and closed and then there was only the silence of the night. The phantom coach had vanished. The poachers hastily departed and when the sun came up a crumpled body was found dumped on the front doorstep of the empty hall. It was George Mace. Not a mark of murder was on him but in his lifeless

ABOVE - *the gaunt and lonely ruins of Egmere church in north Norfolk where a band of phantom pilgrims pass by on their way to Walsingham.*

eyes there was a look of terror. The ghostly drivers of these phantom coaches which charge around East Anglia during darkness pay little heed to the dumb animals' humble petition in Langham church porch which pleads -

Rest, drivers rest, on this steep hill,
Dumb beasts, pray use, with all good will.
Goad not, scourge not, with thonged whips,
Let not one curse escape your lips.
God sees and hears.

Being headless, perhaps the coachmen can neither curse nor read.

Ghosts of gibbeted highwaymen wander the London road near the pine-topped tumulus at How Hill while Tutt Hill, a tumulus near Barnham, is the haunt of a traitor's wretched spirit. He was a Saxon who led the Danes by a secret path to capture Thetford. Like the betrayer of St. Benet's Abbey he had been assured that his reward would be higher than his highest hopes. The town was taken, the Saxon's neck was stretched and King Edmund defeated. A nobler, braver Saxon was the one who single-handedly fought the Danes at Balsham. The good thane Oswy, Balsham's lord, was slain at the battle of Ringmere in 1010 and after the Danes had put Thetford to the torch they massacred the villagers of Balsham except for the man who defended himself in the church tower until the Danes went on their way to make a bonfire of Cambridge. The tower of Stethall's Saxon church, which has two bells cast around the time of the Black Death, was used for a ghoulish display in the middle of the last century. The squire shot a burglar, put the body in the belfry and satisfied the morbid curiosity of his neighbours by allowing them to look at the victim for a few pence a time.

The faint tinkling of a bell heralds the approach of a procession of phantom pilgrims treading their eternal path to Walsingham's shrine over the hill near the ruined tower of Egmere church, and the claim that a stormy sea will make the bells of Dunwich's vanished churches toll beneath the waves is an ancient tradition.

117

In 1794 a father and son were hanged at Bury St. Edmunds for murder, the son had killed one of his sisters at the urging of the father. Their young victim was buried in Little Fakenham churchyard, the younger man's body was given to surgeons for dissection in anatomy lessons and the father's was hung in chains at the scene of the murder. Some time later, it is said, a wager was made one night over pints of ale daring one of the drinkers to go to the eerie place where the rotting corpse swung in chains and ask it how it fared. While one man made his way to the dark and lonely spot, his nimble-witted friend ran ahead and hid near the gibbet. When the question was addressed to the murderer's remains, back came the reply in deathly tones, *'I be chilled to the bone and famished summat awful!'* The questioner's retreat, they say, was remarkably rapid. Tales of similar practical jokes are told of other traditional gibbet sites, and many villages have their story of a tipsy reveller falling into a freshly dug grave in the churchyard from which he emerges clutching an old bone to send sober witnesses of his bleary-eyed 'resurrection' fleeing in terror.

There are tales of phantom coaches and devilish hearses vanishing in clouds of steam into the depths of rivers and at Quidenham the peace is disturbed by the funeral procession of an impious squire who ordered his coffin to be carried to the churchyard in the midnight hour by drunken pall-bearers. This irreverent, staggering gang toppled to untimely death in the river and their ghosts are said to regularly re-enact their gurgling moonlight fate. Wandlebury, that haunt of giants, is said to be the home of a phantom warrior who, if challenged, will fight a moonlight battle. A medieval chronicler tells of a knight who floored the spectre and took its horse as his prize but the animal vanished at dawn. The victorious knight was slightly wounded and each year, on the anniversary of the clash, the healed wound re-opened.

Folklore has tales of the stone effigies of long dead knights rising to stretch their limbs numbed by centuries of sleep , a practice, they say, that is betrayed by dusty footprints on the floor! The two stone lions which crouch outside Cambridge's

Fitzwilliam Museum quietly rise when the streets are deserted and pad down into Trumpington Street to quench their thirst with the water that flows along the runnels which once fed Thomas Hobson's market square fountain. He was the inn keeper, carter and town benefactor whose habit of hiring out his horses in strict rotation gave birth to the epithet 'Hobson's choice'.

Above the door of Burrough Green's old school house stand the statues of a boy and girl demurely dressed in costume of Queen Anne's reign - she with mobcap, he with buttoned frock coat and a broad brimmed hat under one arm and both grasping a book. The girl stands beneath an arch inscribed *Train up a child* and over the boy are the words *Naked and ye clothed me*. On May Day eve. when other children are asleep, the statues come to life and climb down to dance on the village green. No one sees their happy prancing or hears their joyful laughter but at dawn there are footprints in the dew. Whether they are ever joined by the de Burghs and their ladies, whose effigies have stared towards heaven in the nearby church for six centuries, legend does not tell, perhaps the rattle of their knightly armour would cause alarm.

Should you think that these old tales of vanishing coaches, devilish soul-snatchers, phantom knights, wide-eyed hounds of hell and spooks of smugglers, highwaymen and queens to be beyond credibility, consider these hauntings or puzzling encounters of recent years. In a Cambridgeshire village which has its own traditional gallows site, a builder, his wife and two young sons moved into a new home and one night the man woke to see a weeping child standing at the foot of his bed. Thinking it was one of his children crying after a nightmare, he rose and the child turned and walked out of the bedroom. When he reached the landing there was no sign of the child but he noticed that all the lights were on. He looked into his sons' bedrooms and all was quiet, they were sleeping soundly in their beds. Downstairs, too, the lights were on - but had he not turned off all the lights when he locked up? He checked the doors, turned off the lights and returned to bed. The next day he asked if anyone had been up in the night. No, none of the family had stirred but his youngest son inquired, 'Daddy, why were you scratching on the door last night?' The land on which their new house stood had been, many years before, the site of an old cottage in which a child had died when the thatch caught fire.

A Suffolk policeman whose beat took him past an isolated church, noticed that lights were on in the building late one night and as he approached he could hear the organ being

ABOVE - *the stone boy and girl in rustic early 18th century dress on Burrough Green School. On May Day eve they are said to climb down and dance on the village green.*

played. Suddenly the lights went out and the music ceased. The organist had obviously finished his practice. The constable walked up the path through the silent churchyard, checked the doors and found that the unseen organist had securely locked up behind him. The policeman thought no more of the midnight music until the next morning when he looked in the church and to his surprise he found the organ in pieces - dismantled, dusty and piled to one side awaiting restoration.

A Methodist minister was driving through a small Suffolk village one night when suddenly a dog dashed out into the road in front of him. He could not avoid hitting the animal and he felt the wheels on the driver's side of the car go up and over the dog's body. He stopped and expected to find a dead animal in the road, but there was nothing - no dog, no marks, no dent in the car. He noticed a man standing at a nearby bus shelter so the minister approached him to ask if he had witnessed the incident. 'Were it an old black dog?' queried the man. The minister said that it was and he described how he had felt the car go over the beast. 'Don't you worry none 'bout that, it happens here regular.' was the man's reply.

A Norfolk businessman was driving home late one autumn Friday night when suddenly the car headlights picked out a grey figure striding along the road. He swerved, muttered a curse about stupid pedestrians walking in the middle of the road at night and continued on his way. Two miles further on it happened again, a man in a long grey coat was hurriedly pacing along the road. The driver reached home and as he was about to unlock his front door something caught his eye. It was the grey figure marching silently down the village street. A few seconds later the figure vanished and there was a sound and a glint of light from across the road. The next morning the man was in his garden when he heard a familiar sound. It was the same sound that he had heard the previous night. It was the rusty creak of the churchyard gate across the road as some ladies carried flowers and fruit into the church for harvest festival.

Index of Place Names

Index of Place Names

Index of Place Names

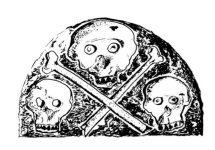